# PRAISE FOR *START WITH AMEN*

"From the first to the last pages of *Start with Amen*, you will see how God links his dream for us to his vision through us! You will experience new thirst and expectancy for receiving the 'hidden wealth of the secret places' (Isa. 45:3) and realize—I pray as never before—that for you, just as for Beth, *the secret place is the secret* to life in all its fullest. As you review the subtitles of every chapter and get to the very last, imagine there is an added chapter—an epilogue—that you yourself will write as your part of this story, and its subtitle is this: *The Invitation of Amen*! I pray your RSVP says 'YES!'"

—Dr. Susan Hillis

Speaker, author, captain in US Public Health Service

"*Start with Amen* was an inspiration and eye opener. For me, the word *amen* is used to describe something I do to close a prayer or offer thanks. But as she points out so eloquently, it was intended to describe a spiritual position before God—a start of something, not just an ending. This book is part study of the Scriptures, part illustrations—with real life examples—that bring to life practical ways to put Scripture to work, and a whole lot of inspiration. Prepare to be challenged. Beth constructs *Start with Amen* in a way that inspires you to not fall into orphan thinking but to realize that God cares about *everything* you do. A great read for those looking to go deeper with God and to be inspired by someone who lives that out every day."

—Kirk Perry

President of brand solutions, Google

"All my life I've prayed and put a period at the end of *amen*. After reading *Start with Amen*, I've experienced a new revelation about how to begin my conversations with God. Beth Guckenberger leads you through the practice of beginning with the end and how it immediately aligns your will with his. Sacred in every way, she testifies that this place of oneness is where even what can't be seen causes your heart to swell with supernatural confidence and hope. Beautiful and praiseworthy, this work is filled with the immeasurable possibilities that follow when you utter your *amen* to God *first*—for his glory and his glory alone."

—Tami Heim

President & CEO, Christian Leadership Alliance

"I have seen firsthand the fruit of Beth's prayers. I have spent time with her and her husband in Monterrey, Mexico, and I've seen the way that Back2Back has made an impact all over the world. Beth's heart is always open to God and his love for those who have been pushed to the margins in our society. In 2007 I rode my bicycle across the country to benefit orphans. That trip was born out of one of Beth's prayers that I would let God use me in a way that went far beyond what I could dream or ever expect of myself. Beth makes space for God in every aspect of her daily life, and these prayers are born in that sacred space. They are prayers that change lives, including mine."

—Mark Schultz

Dove Award winner

"Amid the noise of a groaning world and our own aching hearts, Beth Guckenberger helps us hear the Heartbeat at the center of the universe, pulsing with love and mercy. The guidance Beth offers is not speculation; it is godly wisdom rough-hewn from the sorrows, sacrifices, and joys found only in long journeys of faith, near to the heart of Jesus."

—Jedd Medefind

President, Christian Alliance for Orphans

Author of *Becoming Home*

"Beth is an amazing storyteller, and this book is no exception. She has a wonderful knack for captivating the reader with her personal life stories and intertwining them with the timeless treasures of God's Word."

—Lonnie Clouse

NASCAR chaplain with Motor Racing Outreach

"In her new book, *Start with Amen*, Beth unpacks Old Testament and New Testament truth about our covenant-making, promise-keeping God, who can be trusted with our full lives surrendered to his ways. Beth, through incredible story, personal transparency, and intimacy with Jesus, walks the reader to the place of freedom and power that Christ intends for us to enjoy. Beth's book is a proclamation of what surrender and unflinching obedience to the God of all power can yield in the life of the reader. . . . Enter this book with great expectancy to experience greater faith, new hope, freedom from fear, and a fresh ability to trust our all-loving God."

—Steve Biondo

Senior vice president, Family Christian

"While reading *Start With Amen*, I realized how much my mind and heart needed reconditioning. Like hair that gets dry and brittle from overexposure, so my spiritual walk needed this reboot and reminder that God waits to do life for us and through us. Our energy needs to be refocused on resting in his provision. Starting our days, our appointments, our challenges with *amen* helps us orient our minds and wills to let God be the 'I am' in the everyday. Thanks, Beth, for being used of the Spirit to comfort, convict, and clarify in this profoundly simple revelation."

—Emilie Wierda
President, Eagle Companies
Bible Teacher, mom, seminarian

# START
# WITH
# AMEN

# START WITH AMEN

## How I Learned to Surrender by Keeping the End in Mind

## BETH GUCKENBERGER

W PUBLISHING GROUP

AN IMPRINT OF THOMAS NELSON

Published in Nashville, Tennessee, by W Publishing, an imprint of Thomas Nelson.

Published in association with Alive Communications, Inc., 7680 Goddard Street, Suite 200, Colorado Springs, CO 80920. www.alivecommunications.com

Thomas Nelson titles may be purchased in bulk for educational, business, fund-raising, or sales promotional use. For information, please e-mail SpecialMarkets@ThomasNelson.com.

Any Internet addresses, phone numbers, or company or product information printed in this book are offered as a resource and are not intended in any way to be or to imply an endorsement by Thomas Nelson, nor does Thomas Nelson vouch for the existence, content, or services of these sites, phone numbers, companies, or products beyond the life of this book.

Unless otherwise noted, Scripture quotations are taken from the Holy Bible, New International Version®, NIV®. Copyright © 1973, 1978, 1984, 2011 by Biblica, Inc.® Used by permission of Zondervan. All rights reserved worldwide. www.zondervan.com. The "NIV" and "New International Version" are trademarks registered in the United States Patent and Trademark Office by Biblica, Inc.®

Scripture quotations marked ASV are from the Authorized Standard Version. Public domain.

Scripture quotations marked ESV are from the ESV® Bible (The Holy Bible, English Standard Version®). Copyright © 2001 by Crossway, a publishing ministry of Good News Publishers. Used by permission. All rights reserved.

Scripture quotations marked THE MESSAGE are from The Message. Copyright © by Eugene H. Peterson 1993, 1994, 1995, 1996, 2000, 2001, 2002. Used by permission of Tyndale House Publishers, Inc.

Scripture quotations marked NASB are from New American Standard Bible®. Copyright © 1960, 1962, 1963, 1968, 1971, 1972, 1973, 1975, 1977, 1995 by The Lockman Foundation. Used by permission. (www.Lockman.org)

Scripture quotations marked NKJV are from the New King James Version®. © 1982 by Thomas Nelson. Used by permission. All rights reserved.

Scripture quotations marked NLT are from the Holy Bible, New Living Translation. © 1996, 2004, 2007, 2013 by Tyndale House Foundation. Used by permission of Tyndale House Publishers, Inc., Carol Stream, Illinois 60188. All rights reserved.

Scripture quotations marked NRSV are from New Revised Standard Version Bible. Copyright © 1989 National Council of the Churches of Christ in the United States of America. Used by permission. All rights reserved.

Unless otherwise noted, italics in Scripture are the author's emphasis.

ISBN 978-0-7180-7901-7 (SC)
ISBN 978-0-8540-7 (eBook)

**Library of Congress Cataloging-in-Publication Data**

Names: Guckenberger, Beth, 1972- author.
Title: Start with amen : how I learned to surrender by keeping the end in
  mind / Beth Guckenberger.
Description: Nashville : W Publishing Group, 2017. | Includes bibliographical
  references.
Identifiers: LCCN 2016053325 | ISBN 9780718079017 (trade paper)
Subjects: LCSH: Prayer--Christianity. | Submissiveness--Religious
  aspects--Christianity.
Classification: LCC BV210.3 .G83 2017 | DDC 248.3/2--dc23 LC record available at https://lccn.loc.gov/2016053325

*Printed in the United States of America*

17 18 19 20 21  LSC  10 9 8 7 6 5 4 3 2 1

*To my mom, Ruth Ewing:*
*I have a thousand memories of your Bible open on*
*our kitchen table. Thank you for teaching me about*
*the rock from which I was cut. After a lifetime of*
*your influence, I know for sure: presence matters.*

For all the promises of God find their Yes in him. That is why it is through him that we utter our Amen to God for his glory.

—2 Corinthians 1:20 ESV

**a·men**

/äˈmen, āˈmen/

*exclamation*

   1. uttered at the end of a prayer or hymn, meaning "so be it."[1]

# CONTENTS

# CONTENT

# PROLOGUE

The week before I was headed out of town, the usual anxiety crept in. *Should I be going? Did I hear this assignment right? Am I one mess-up from a disaster, and this might be it?*

I woke up straight from a dream so real I knew right away it was from the Lord. There was a heaviness about it, and it was in Technicolor, the way Jesus dreams seem to be. I was building a bridge across a rushing river, but I had run out of materials, which left me stranded. I seemed unsure of what to do next. How was I going to get to the other side?

In the morning, I recounted it to my husband, Todd, and we assumed it was about our impending adoption. Many times I had expressed how in-over-our-heads I felt about it. Todd mentioned maybe I was to pray for more "materials." This explanation satisfied me, and I didn't think about it again.

Later in the same week, I left to speak at an adoption conference. It was a heavy season of "going," and my metaphorical cup was not feeling full. The needs of the women in the room weighed on me, and I dreaded walking into dozens of conversations with questions I didn't feel equipped to answer. I closed my remarks, and within minutes, women came forward, mostly for prayer. Normally, I love this, but today it felt overwhelming.

A woman made her way to the front, leading with, "Beth, there's something I *have* to tell you . . ." I felt myself shrink, but she didn't seem to notice. "While you were speaking, I had a vision. It was of you building a bridge over some sort of danger-ous river, but you didn't have enough material to finish it." The typical bustle of an emptying-out ballroom faded, and her voice pierced my fatigue.

I grabbed her hand, and we found a quiet corner. "I had that same dream just this week. I thought it was about something else, but . . ." My voice trailed off as my mind caught up to how weird this was. "Who *are* you?"

Her name was Dr. Susan Hillis, and she worked for the Centers for Disease Control as a global health adviser special-izing in the orphan crisis. She told me the Lord had given her the picture of the bridge many times over the last two years. She believed it was tied to the passage in Ephesians: "I keep asking that the God of our Lord Jesus Christ, the glorious Father, may give you the Spirit of wisdom and revelation, so that you may know him better" (1:17).

"Wisdom is the entire truth of God and all that he has cre-ated. Revelation is the sweet whisper of the Holy Spirit we hear behind us, saying, 'This is the way; walk in it.'" She looked at me as if this should all make sense. (I wasn't sure it did.) "If the bridge stops in the middle of the river, we are only walking in wisdom or only walking in revelation."

I was sure she meant *me* when she said *we*.

"Beth, you can't be caught halfway," Susan implored. "The

river below is too dangerous and the stakes too high. You need them both to take others across."

I knew Susan and I had a divine date orchestrated by God himself, but what could this mean? We ended up talking all afternoon about something she called the "orphan spirit."

An orphan spirit isn't experienced exclusively by orphans; it's a sense in any of us that we need to earn God's favor. It's coming to God with a "pretty please give me what I ask for so I believe you like me" attitude. It's the daughter of a plantation owner, but it acts like a slave, begging at the master's door for a scrap.

The orphan spirit smells of duty and shame. It self-rejects and seeks comfort in counterfeit affections. It's competitive and makes everyone a rival. It's guarded and conditional, living in bondage and fighting for what it can get. It's unbridled sin crouching at the metaphorical door, desiring to master its host. It lacks spiritual confidence because it thinks we need to earn favor, and there is no way to ever satisfy our debt.

God is our chief teacher and is always the loudest voice in the room. He might use a conversation and someone else's voice, but when he is authoring the content, your spirit just knows. It leaps in response. God knows what I need to learn and uses whatever vessel he wants to bring me his truth. Some days, he teaches me a lesson through a child; other days, through a song, his creation, or a well-timed message. Today, he used this energetic new friend. *We have to live like daughters.* It's critical to our surrender.

The orphan spirit is diverse in its host, from the well-established professional who can't ever seem to work enough to the parent who frantically makes her children her god. It's in the person who never commits, jumping from relationship to relationship, or who has addictions he is never able to manage.

"The orphan spirit looks to land where we allow it." Susan leaned in conspiratorially. "It is *the* epidemic crisis spreading exponentially across the globe."

I shook my head. I wanted to have a clever answer. Or better yet, a plan. I knew God wanted me to hear this; the dream led me to this conversation. I sat quietly, processing.

"Do you know how many children around the world have been abused, meaning assaulted physically, verbally, emotionally, sexually?" She pulled off her glasses and dared me to respond.

At this point, I had nothing. God hadn't told me that in any dream.

"One billion. Of the two billion children in the world today, half of them have been compromised."[1]

Had God thought this conversation would be better for me than a dozen versions of small talk? I prayed at some level, although there were no words. It's amazing how we can just sit in the bigness of a message and feel overwhelmed by the Spirit and not know what it's for. I was searching for something to say, but all that came to mind was profanity.

Susan looked at me, expectant. There was a long pause, and I felt desperate to fill it.

Finally, I whispered, "Amen," and the word was pregnant with meaning. It was simultaneously an affirmation of her message and a release of tension as I handed this conversation over to the Lord. I remember thanking her and looking for the exit. I slipped into my hotel room and sat on the bed with my legs crossed and my Bible open.

*Orphan spirit. Bridges without enough material. One billion children. Counterfeit affections.*

"What do you want from me, Lord?" I bowed my head and spoke out loud. "I trust you. I trust you are still God, even though one billion of your littlest people are hurting. What will you do? What can you do? What should you do? What is there to do? I don't even know which question to ask. What do you want me to do? This orphan spirit is just the by-product of an ongoing attack on your creation. We live in brokenness. I am broken. Amen! We need your strength. *I* need your strength. Amen! Come for us, dear Jesus."

I don't know how long I sat there, waiting for him to answer. It takes more discipline than I would like to sit and be still. I prefer to war with another or, even better, war against the world, but the most intimate of wars happen within my own head.

Lamentations came to mind:

I remember my affliction and my wandering . . .
I well remember them,
    and my soul is downcast within me.
*Yet this I call to mind*
    *and therefore I have hope:*

Because of the LORD's great love we are not consumed,
    for his compassions never fail.
They are new every morning;
    great is your faithfulness.
I say to myself, "The LORD is my portion;
    therefore I will wait for him."
The LORD is good to those whose hope is in him,
    to the one who seeks him. (3:19–25)

Prayer is a discipline, not just a conversation. I willed my thoughts into submission. *Yet this I call to mind and therefore I have hope.*

And my spiritual confidence swelled. I had no more answers than I did an hour or so before, but I was reminded anew that God is on the move. The tears fell, but they felt more like a spiritual bath than an emotional release. He *is* a communicative God. He longs to impress upon us his presence, the very opposite of an orphan spirit. He wants to give us his good gifts so we can turn around and share those good gifts with others. As I wrestled with God that afternoon (*teach me, show me, help me, use me*), I confessed the one billion are his responsibility, not mine.

As for me? I am to live and love like a daughter, talk like a daughter. I am to invite and extend myself and risk. Life's sweetest tastes come from risk. I am to root myself in his identity and not gorge myself on counterfeit affections. I am then to testify every chance I get: freedom is found in forfeiting my own way.

*Amen.*

This is that testimony.

# CHAPTER 1

# SO BE IT

## *The Posture of Amen*

*Ezra praised the LORD, the great God; and all the
people lifted their hands and responded, "Amen!
Amen!" Then they bowed down and worshipped
the LORD with their faces to the ground.*

—NEHEMIAH 8:6

I sat on the Mount of Olives and gazed at Jerusalem's Old City.
I noticed the series of gates built and boarded up in the centuries since Jesus walked there. The gates rest on Bible stories
we've read hundreds of times, yet the meaning of the architec-
ture seems to have gotten lost. These ancient entryways were
once specific points of passage for kings and commoners, for
merchants and grand processions, guarded through the centuries by tradition and diplomacy.

Among them was a tiny sheep gate. First mentioned in the book of Nehemiah, it was the entrance for sheep used in sacrifices. The door is clearly much smaller than the other gates, and although no animal was passing through it on that day, I imagined a line of sheep, wrapped around the city, being brought in for major Jewish holidays. Sheep as far as the eye could see. According to the Jewish historian Josephus, almost a quarter million animals walked through the thin gate during the Passover week, the week of Jesus' death.[1]

Imagining Jesus coming down the hill on Palm Sunday, with everyone waving their branches, I wondered where he entered. The Bible doesn't tell us, but I can't imagine Herod would have let Jesus enter through his gate. I stared for a while at the walls. He was a king who became a common man who then became the sacrificial lamb. So how did he enter this city?

Whether Jesus went through this particular gate or not, his was the sheep's gate.

Later in the afternoon, we visited a Greek ruin. I couldn't stop taking pictures of the extraordinary buildings: enormous theaters and coliseums, bathhouses and schools.

I stood on one of those wide roads, mouth open, sketching what I saw, being so impressed with what man could do. My mind flitted back to the scene of the gates earlier in the day, and, for a second, a verse ran through my head.

"Enter through the narrow gate. For wide is the gate and broad is the road that leads to destruction, and many enter through it. But small is the gate and narrow the road that leads to life, and only a few find it." (Matt. 7:13–14)

It was as if God had posed the sweetest of questions. *You want to be impressed with what man can do? That's your choice, but it will lead to your own destruction.*

*If you want life—real life—follow me. I'll be entering the city through the narrow gate.*

*Together, we will be laying down our lives.*

I sighed as I realized that a sheep gate awaits me every day. Above it hangs a sign: "This is the Way. Surrender." Through it I find blessings I never imagined, as sacrifice reveals itself as the entry point for peace. Jesus found shalom in obedience to the will of the Father and has been inviting us to discover the same ever since.

I want the peace. I want to not worry when circumstances or relationships induce panic. I want the latest incident to be my excuse to exercise a growing muscle in me that says, *Amen.* As I cross the sheep gate threshold, this little word means, *So be it. I trust you. I don't understand, but I surrender. It's in your hands now.*

## WHEN AMEN TOOK OVER

In 1997, my husband, Todd, and I moved to Monterrey, Mexico, to serve orphans and vulnerable children full-time through Back2Back Ministries. Living in a developing country for a long time means you exponentially increase your odds of being robbed. It's not unusual, and you take extra precautions, but the risk is still there. I say this because it was a ridiculous purchase. As a missionary, I had long carried purses that looked like a combination of army backpack and bohemian sling bag. Why

I lusted one day for a purple Coach purse in the window of a Texas outlet is still a mystery to me. That light-lilac suede was so impractical. I didn't even wear much purple, but I am sure it symbolized something to me about another world I could live in if I wanted.

I was at my son's soccer game when it was stolen. Someone shattered the window in my car and snatched it a few feet from where I stood. I should've panicked about the credit cards that needed to be canceled or the cell phone I could've used to call for help or the pictures of my children I carried in my wallet. But I immediately started grieving the loss of the purse.

After making some police reports, I went home and commandeered my nine-year-old daughter's dress-up purse and used it for the next month, knowing soon I would be flying into the United States and could replace it with something more practical. I vowed *never again* to the purple purse.

I flew into Cincinnati, Ohio, weeks later and had only one hour before a speaking engagement, so I searched a nearby strip mall to see if I could quickly pick up a new purse.

My only option was a luggage store. I stepped in and saw a rack with cool leather backpack purses, a bit of a hybrid between my earlier choices and the Coach. I had never heard of the brand, but it looked nice and sturdy, so I took it to the counter.

"That'll be $276," the lady said, ringing my purchase into her cash register.

My eyes went wide at the price, I muttered, "No, thank you," and left the store. I didn't think about it again, as now I was late to my engagement. I pulled into the place where I was meeting the others, grabbed Emma's ratty purse, and told the Lord I understood my roots.

I knew he didn't value or care about purses, and neither would I.

Finally, the evening's event was over, and I headed to my mom's house, where I was staying for a few days. I settled into my childhood room and looked over mail accumulated since our last visit. I'd had a birthday since my previous trip to the States, and I sat on the edge of the bed, reading cards. At the bottom of the mailbag, there was a package from my college friend, who had remembered my birthday and sent a gift to my mom's house. I thought fondly of her as I opened the box, and then threw my hands to my mouth when I saw what was inside.

It was my $276 leather backpack purse. Exact. Same. One.

A flood of thoughts came over me as I held it.

She and I had never exchanged gifts so generous before.

She didn't know about the theft, did she?

Is this for real? God picked this out for me *before* I wanted it today?

I was so sure he didn't care about designer purses. I had spent a month disciplining my thoughts so I wouldn't grieve something as silly as a purse. Yet here he was, reintroducing me to himself all over again. *I care about everything you care about*, he seemed to say.

That night, before I fell asleep, I thought about all the wasted time I had spent wringing my hands over something God already had in the works to redeem. What if when I didn't like what was happening (a lost purse, broken relationships, poor health, traffic accidents, unexpected bills) I prayed in anticipation of the Lord's hand, confident of his sovereignty? What if instead of second-guessing him, my prayers sounded more like *Amen. So be it. This happened. It's all good. I'm yours. Change my heart. Take captive my thoughts. All I have is in your hands. Bless the thief. Dear Jesus . . . ?*

In this case, I can stretch and pray for the person who took my purse or remind myself mentally of my blessings. I can stretch and be grateful I wasn't assaulted or trust for future provision. What do I gain from worry or, worse yet, fury?

That night, I committed to Jesus that I would rest in the God of Amen.

From now on, I would start our holy conversations by anticipating his hand.

"Amen," I began before any other words followed.

## AMEN IS COMPLETE DEPENDENCE

Back to Israel. Our guide, Bible teacher Ray Vander Laan, took us to a hill where we watched sheep graze under the careful eye of their shepherd. Ray invited us to make observations, and some immediately mentioned the straight line the sheep walk in. They looked like they were playing follow-the-leader. He told us the root word from which we derive the phrase *path of righteousness* is the same root word describing sheep walking in a line. Sheep literally walk along the path of righteousness.

Others commented on the goats that were running around, trying to make their own way and staying off the path of righteousness. Finally, I asked why the shepherd was tending his sheep on a hillside without grass. Everywhere I turned, it seemed brown and rocky.

"Look under the rocks," he encouraged me. "The dew from the morning gets caught under them, and there are small grass clumps that grow. See how the shepherd is walking among his sheep? They know his voice, and he's pointing out to them where the grass is found."

I located the thickest tuft of grass, and it was still smaller than a human fist. Do you know how long it takes to bite, chew, and swallow a small tuft of grass? From our observation, about the time it takes to go three or four steps. Then the sheep has to listen for where he can find the next bite. The sheep stay on the path of righteousness so they are within earshot of a shepherd who is actively pointing out where they can go to get what they need.

I started to think about Psalm 23, and our guide pulled out his Bible. As we talked about the imagery for this passage, we agreed our idea of being led to green pastures conjured up images of waist-high grass, careening in a gentle wind, as far as the eye could see. But my picture of a field of grass represented my total independence. I could eat however much I wanted, whenever I wanted, wherever I wanted. I could tell God thanks beforehand, but all other factors were in my control. David, however, was on hillsides like this rocky one when he penned those words. His idea of God's leading us to a green pasture places us in a posture of dependence, looking more like what I was watching that afternoon. God's way puts me in a position where he might provide only what will sustain me for the next three or four steps. Then, dependent on him for more, I stay on the path within earshot and listen for his leading so I'll find what I need. Listen. Bite. Step. Repeat.

God knows I need to hear his voice more than I need the field of grass. Surrendering to a life of *so be it* is about discerning the difference, holding a posture where I am wholly reliant and deeply committed to believing his voice is the door to provision.

Today, *amen* is most often our sign-off to a prayer or a testimony of agreement, but it was designed to be so much more. Its intent is to describe a spiritual position before God. Nehemiah explains it as: "Ezra praised the LORD, the great God; and all the people lifted their hands and responded, 'Amen! Amen!' Then they bowed down and worshiped the LORD with their faces to the ground" (Neh. 8:6).

This is amen: hands raised, faces bowed, hearts at peace. There our metaphorical spiritual buckets get filled, and there is plenty to offer each other. Unity is felt among the church, and communion is a reality. Here, in this posture, I am always surprised by what God has for me.

If I could pray no other word ever again, I would be okay. *Amen* speaks affirmation and commitment. It says yes to a lifestyle where he is to be trusted and I can rest in him.

When I talk to God, I start with *amen*, and, with it, we communicate intimacy and a sense of knowing.

I know he's *got* this.

He knows I'm letting him *have* this, whatever in the moment "this" may be.

As amen permeated my life and prayers, I noticed a newfound confidence in my faith. I woke up one day along my journey and sensed a fresh boldness in my faith. It wasn't a result of new head knowledge or better self-discipline. It was simply a longing for miracles and revival; I wanted to see God be God. I developed a craving for intimacy with him. This idea of amen, or surrender and submission, opened doors of restoration in my relationships—and in my soul.

But be warned. *Narrow is the path that leads to righteousness.* Developing a faith rooted in amen doesn't come without its roadblocks and diversions. Sometimes it was my sin (and, honestly, sometimes it still is); other times it was another's. We have an enemy, one who seeks to get us as far away from God as possible, to have our lives ruled by chaos and decay.

The way of amen always starts with the Savior, the one who entered through the sheep's gate to make a way for reconciliation with the Father. Because he sacrificed himself, we can say *amen.* Because he showed us what unflinching obedience looks like, we are capable of the same.

God intended this word *amen* to be a moment of intimacy, drenched in reverence, replete with peace—a moment when you rest in him and are rejuvenated by him. He wants to give us so much more.

## AMEN IS OUR RESPONSE
## TO GOD'S COVENANT

God gave up his rights long before the week of Palm Sunday. In Genesis 15, he laid the groundwork for which gate he would one day enter. In order to secure a promise he made to Abram, that he would give him as many children as there are stars in the sky as well as the land in which they would dwell, God made a blood path covenant with him.

Blood path covenants were long the tradition between two parties making a pledge to each other. The Lord could have just said his promise and then expected Abraham to believe it. But he used a practice familiar to Abraham in his cultural context to give him the faith he would need. As was the custom, Abraham would take several animals and split them in half, creating a small, bloody river between the carcasses:

> So the LORD said to him, "Bring me a heifer, a goat and a ram, each three years old, along with a dove and a young pigeon."
>
> Abram brought all these to him, cut them in two and arranged the halves opposite each other; the birds, however, he did not cut in half. (Gen. 15: 9–10)

Then the two parties would walk through the blood path, committing to one another and to the witnesses, "If I break my end of this deal, I will pay the price with my blood." There are all kinds of nuances in these arrangements, but the most important piece is both parties must commit. God knew, however, that Abraham couldn't keep his end of the deal, so the Bible says, "As the sun was setting, Abram fell into a deep sleep, and a thick and dreadful darkness came over him. . . . When the sun had set and darkness had fallen, a smoking firepot with a blazing torch appeared and passed between the pieces" (vv. 12, 17).

God walked through the blood path on behalf of himself *and* Abraham. He was in essence saying, "I will keep this covenant, and if I don't, I will pay the price with my blood. You will keep this covenant, and if you do not, *I* will pay the price with my blood. I would rather my life be divided than break a covenant relationship with you."

The story of which gate Jesus would one day metaphorically enter was put into motion when he walked through the blood path. Theologians call this story a Christophany: the appearance of Christ in the Old Testament. Before they even knew

who Jesus was, his people were set up to understand that someone would pay for their sins in mercy.

Throughout Jewish history, it has been the custom of priests
to offer sacrifices on the altar twice a day, at 9:00 a.m. and 3:00
p.m. We read the instructions of this practice in Exodus 29 and
in Jewish literature.

The 9:00 a.m. and 3:00 p.m. ritual would have been active
on Good Friday, when Jesus entered into the city as the sheep
and not the king. Mark 15 tells us Jesus was put on the cross at
9:00 a.m.—when the first sacrifice was being made.

There he hung for six hours.

This doesn't make any sense. If I were Jesus, I might have
said, around 1:30 in the afternoon, "Enough! I will still die and
resurrect, I will still conquer death, and I will still have people
tell my story, but not one minute more!"

Instead, in Matthew 27, we see a Savior who held out until
orchestrating his own death perfectly at 3:00 p.m.

God does not deal in coincidences. He was proving a point.
He was fulfilling a promise he had made long before.

This is a God who is always *perfectly* on time. This is a
Savior who shows what a life of *amen* means—unflinching obedience and power in sacrifice. His life has long been defining
what keeping a promise looks like.

So why do I doubt him? Why do some days I pout over something not happening fast enough, knowing full well that he is
actively working so those details will unfold perfectly in his time?
I doubt because in that moment I have not surrendered. I might
pray, but they are words strung together designed to manipulate
a holy God to adjust to my will. I will finish the prayer with
*amen*, but I don't mean, "So be it." I mean, *"So do it."*

*Amen* is the verbal equivalent of hands raised. It can be translated as "So be it" or paraphrased as "It is as you say." It's more than our modern understanding of "uncle" or "I give up." It is surrender in a spirit of "It's up to you; you do it," and "I made the promise, but only you can fulfill it." So I whisper, *You sell the house. You move her heart. You heal that body. You open the door. You provide. You go before them. Amen. So be it. In your time. I trust. I surrender. Amen.*

And this one word reorients me, calibrating me with a God whose covenant he will never break.

## START WITH THE ENDING

*Amen* is a word found in virtually all languages around the globe, originating in Hebrew and then brought by Paul and the missionaries to the Greek world. The Greeks didn't have a translation for it, so they just adopted it, and cultures have been following suit ever since. Wherever faithful people gather, you can be sure to hear it uttered in affirmation and in conclusion of their time in prayer.

When I am in conversation with Jesus, I really do want my first soul steps to be, *"Yes, so be it. It is as you say . . ."* Otherwise, I can too easily start down a path where I am whining or begging or negotiating or accusing. Beginning with *amen* sets my pace as I go down that path; it stills my heart and reminds me with whom I am talking.

Jesus often began his comments with the Hebrew word *amen*, which is translated in the Gospels as "truly" or "verily" nearly seventy times. In John 3, when Jesus was talking to

Nicodemus, he said literally, "[Amen, amen] I say to you, unless one is born again he cannot see the kingdom of God" (v. 3 NASB). Whereas prophets had to declare, "Thus says the Lord," Jesus simply acknowledged his own authority, "Amen, I say to you . . ." His words were the truth, and just by him saying them, we could have confidence *in* them.

That's what I'm looking for: a spiritual confidence that supersedes circumstances, a peace that passes understanding (Phil. 4:7). These are promises accessible to me on earth, and the barrier between those promises and my reality lies in direct correlation to how quickly I acknowledge, "So be it. It is as you say." The slower I am to get to *amen*, the more painful my faith journey seems. In contrast, the more this word passes my lips, the lower my knees sink, landing me in the peace I long for.

Starting off with *amen* dates as far back as the prophets.

> Then the prophet Jeremiah replied to the prophet Hananiah before the priests and all the people who were standing in the house of the LORD. He said, "Amen! May the LORD do so! May the LORD fulfill the words you have prophesied by bringing the articles of the LORD's house and all the exiles back to this place from Babylon." (Jer. 28:5–6)

"Amen! May the Lord do so . . ." What if I spent more time trusting the Lord will do this and less time wrestling with him? Isaiah 65:16 reads, "Because he who is blessed in the earth will be blessed by the God of truth" (NASB). Using the original language, this verse could also be translated, "He who is blessed in the earth will be blessed by the God of *Amen*." This word has long been less of a sign-off and more of an avowal.

Each time I say *amen*, it's like lifting a huge barbell with my faith muscle. It simply makes me stronger. *Amen. You are to be trusted. Amen. You do have a plan. Amen. So be it. I surrender.* Each time I use it, my muscle rips and grows, enabling me to lift a truth or a reality I couldn't before. When I start my time with *amen*, it eliminates my transactional conversations with him as I recognize more quickly, who am I to make deals with God?

*Amen* is also used as a descriptor of God. John shares in Revelation 3:14, "To the angel of the church in Laodicea write: These are the words *of the Amen, the faithful and true witness*, the ruler of God's creation." This gives me hope. I need a relationship with someone who will be faithful. I want to trust his witness is not false, and I am grateful someone is ruling this creation because I need to talk to him.

I watch as daily life slams against a theology of amen I long to live by. Will I believe it to be true? Will it give me hope? Does it have enough grit to sustain me when I am tired or afraid? When a calling stalls or someone wounds me, God promises, "He is before all things, and in him all things hold together" (Col. 1:17). When my own sin disrupts a relationship, amen. I can raise that barbell over my head and say, "'There is therefore now no condemnation'" (Rom. 8:1 ESV). Knowing he is the faithful and true witness helps me hold on to his words.

Living amen is a sacred rhythm. It is surrender to sovereignty in all circumstances. The result is a rapport with the living God so intense it permeates everything. It affects how I talk to my husband, interact with neighbors, spend money, make plans, and raise my kids. It influences how affected I am by other people's thoughts of me or someone else's crisis. It's the antidote to fear and control when they raise their heads in my thoughts. Surrendering to a life of *so be it* is an acknowledgment that my knee is bowed and someone else is on the throne. I care about who holds a political office, but I don't have confidence in it. I can cry over a difficult news story, but I trust he is using it for his glory. With my limited human understanding, I wonder how he allows all that he does, but whether I am shaking my fist or holding up my hand, the same will always be true: he has forever been and forever will be the King.

Typically when we pray, we start with *Dear Jesus*, and requests or confessions follow. I have lots of both. I want things for myself, my family, and this world. I am always telling him what I want. I confess to him thoughts not held captive and carnal intentions I struggle to control. By starting with *amen*, I get to sing the song of "It's all good" throughout the prayer.

If I get what I want (for myself, my family, or this world), wow. It's all good. Thank you, Lord.

If I don't get what I want (children stay sick, planes stay grounded, governments continue to wage war), it's all good. He is in control. I can trust. Thank you, Lord.

When we start our holy conversations with the spirit of *so be it*, we say, "I trust you. I hope in you. I yield." And then, knowing we can't sustain that kind of courage on our own, we have to finish the prayer with the plea of *Dear Jesus*.

Just to be clear, "It's all good" is not the same as "I'm fine." I'm fine is a defense mechanism, another way to say, "It doesn't matter." (It does to him.)

"You wouldn't care." (He does.)

"You aren't worth it." (He is, and so are you.)

"I don't want to deal with it." (We need to.)

My friend Emilee told me once, when I answered her question

with "I'm fine," that *fine* is the Christian f-word. Spiritual confidence isn't rooted in "I'm fine," which looks like gritted teeth,
a plastic smile, and glazed-over eyes. Spiritual confidence is
rooted in "It's all good," which means, "Thank goodness I can
trust him who is in control, because clearly I am not."

As we train ourselves in a life of *amen* first, we experience
tremendous benefits: intimacy with God and others, the reward
of abundant grace and peace, reconciled relationships, and less
overall human drama. Mostly, walking in abandon results in
being reintroduced to this multifaceted God over and over again.

In my relationship with Jesus, there have been seasons of
passionate interaction and newlywed-like infatuation—and
other periods of cooling off, when I dabbled my toes in waters
where they didn't belong. I have wrestled with him over circumstances, stomped my feet over loss, questioned him in my doubt,
and clung to him during brokenness. If there is something you
can ask of or about Jesus, I've done it. I'm spiritual by nature,
and I am always stirring the soul waters inside.

I don't know the exact moment when it happened, this
crossing over from believing in God to believing God, although
I now know I don't want to go back. I have finally settled myself
at his feet. Some days I feel anticipation, so I stand there on
tiptoes. Some days I feel exhausted, so I am facedown, without
words. On days with questions, I raise my hand. On days of
celebration, I dance spiritually like I wish I could physically. I
have decided to permanently take up residence in the throne
room, heart rendered to his sovereignty. If this spiritual posture
could talk, it would say, "Amen. So be it."

# CHAPTER 2

# POSITION OF PROXIMITY

## *The Benefit of Amen*

*The LORD came down on Mount Sinai, to the top
of the mountain; and the LORD called Moses to
the top of the mountain, and Moses went up.*

—EXODUS 19:20 NASB

I remember the day it all started: this sense that borders were
mine for the crossing and children everywhere deserved
permanency. It was supposed to be just a week, something to
experience. I had no idea on this summer afternoon in 1996 that
everything would shift to the point that I would never again live
as I had before.

Todd and I were young with plenty of discretionary time, and we volunteered as sponsors in our local youth ministry. Part of that privilege was to accompany students on the annual summer mission trip to Mexico, serving a church there. The mission wasn't clear, but that didn't matter at the time, as we set to work diligently repainting the blue wall that surrounded the church a nice shade of green. The only problem was, I am pretty sure, if my memory serves correctly, the year before we had painted a green wall blue.

On the second-to-last day, Todd worked hard edging the wall where it met the gate, like the gate was in heaven itself, but I complained about the week-long paint project. I think he was tired of my dramatic grumbling, so he interrupted my endless chatter long enough to ask, "Do you remember the orphanage we visited in Albania?"

"Do I remember? Yes, of course I remember. Why?" We had spent a few weeks there in college with the ministry Cru, and it had made a distinct impression on us.

"Do you think there are any here in this town?" he asked.

Most of life's best stories start with questions you don't have the answer to, and this was no exception. It didn't take much to coax me away from the paint project, so with little more than some gumption we jumped in a taxi, looking for a holy plan B.

"Orphanage-o? Orphanatorio? Orphanagorio?" I tried saying every combination with my best Spanish accent to communicate with the driver.

I'm not sure what we were thinking. We didn't speak Spanish, didn't have enough pesos to get us back to the students, and didn't know the name of the street the church was on. We should have panicked. However, an hour later as we landed in front of an orphanage on a dusty road and knocked at the door, we felt at peace.

Through some very creative communication, we were able to tell the director we had three things: two hundred US dollars, twenty-five high school students, and one day left on our trip. Then we asked, "If you had access to those resources, what would you use them for?"

I had never asked a question like that before. I felt like a bridge, and I really wanted this man and the kids peeking out from behind him to walk across me. There was a longing in me for something, but I didn't know how to discern what it was at the time. Was it longing for them to have what they needed? A longing for me to be used? For the kids we brought to be a part of something? A longing for God to be known? Yes to all of the above. I am sure there was a mix of my holiness and self-centeredness all mashed together.

The director of the home answered softly, "The children haven't had meat in over a year, and the window up there is broken."

A sympathetic "Wow" escaped my lips. I felt like God was playing a cosmic game of truth or dare, and it was his turn. After a lifetime of truth, he was daring us to engage.

"See you tomorrow," we promised as we backed away from the house, the rawness of the moment leaving us breathless.

The next day, we brought a new window and a couple hundred hamburgers.

After Todd had finished his repairs, he checked in with me at the grill. "Do you see that little girl?" He pointed out a preschooler whose cheeks were puffed out from a huge bite of burger she had just taken.

"I can't keep my eyes off her. Isn't she so cute?" I replied, not making eye contact with him, still prepping burgers on the table.

"Well, I am pretty sure you've taken your eyes off her a time or two because I have seen her take four hamburgers from you. I don't know any little girl who can put that down. Why don't you follow her and see where she's taking the burgers?"

As she came to the table again, I gave her a burger and took her hand. Following this little girl, I could tell she was leading me somewhere. I just didn't know where.

When we reached the doorframe of her dorm room, she hesitated only slightly as she turned to look at me. Then, dropping my grip, she scampered over to her friends. There she joined them as they lifted their mattresses, hiding the meat underneath, saving it for later.

*Wow,* I thought for the second time in two days. It felt like a holy sucker punch. I called Todd over to that doorframe, and we had a conversation that marked my life in ways I can hardly describe here. We talked about people we knew who would buy kids hamburgers if they only understood how to get them there.

We've since called that conversation our defining moment. I had no idea at the time—I wish it would've been painted across the sky: "You have just wrecked everything"—but that's not how it works. There was simply this compulsion to change our lives, or at least shift them. *Shift* sounds sweeter somehow than *change,* which implies there is an ugly "before" picture and a forthcoming "after." We were somewhere in the middle between the before and after, and the transformation that needed to happen next is the kindness of God, who won't leave us where he finds us.

The shift was blown by a wind whispering to us what we were capable of and where God wanted us to invest our time and talent. There was a supernatural aspect to this moving of priorities, and I was sure the story to come was bigger than we could've ever written on our own.

There was nothing particularly bad about my life before that moment. I was not doing anything so wrong that the shift was a discipline or a correction. It was more like a big wooden marker in the shape of an arrow pointing to somewhere I couldn't see but was excited to explore.

We came home and wondered what *set* looked like in the *ready, set, go* posture. We felt ready to do something and were interested in going, but *set* seemed critical. We bought a map of Mexico and hung it on our kitchen wall, and as we were in this simple season of double income and no kids, we saved one salary in the bank account and lived off the other. Surely, that must be what *set* looks like.

We finished that year and were sitting on a treasure. It was one year of a teaching salary, but it was more money than I had ever had before. It certainly felt like enough money to let us move to Mexico. Our plan was to carry that money in a safe and live off it as long as it lasted. I went to the local bank and asked to withdraw all our funds, but that alerted the bank manager. After a lengthy conversation, he talked me into buying traveler's checks for the entire amount.

We left on July 1, 1997, for what we thought would be a year, and within the first week we went to the local bank to turn those traveler's checks into pesos. The cashier was giving me instructions I couldn't understand, and I tried guessing what she was insisting on. She talked slow and loud, but we still weren't connecting. I passed her my passport, but that wasn't right. I tried charades and prayer, but nothing worked. We were at an impasse. If these checks didn't turn into pesos, we couldn't even buy gas to get back to Ohio. I looked at her wild-eyed, ready to reach over the counter and grab what I needed.

She could tell I was escalating, and she matched me, practically shouting now for the twentieth time, "*¡Tienes que firmar tu nombre aqui!*"

*Oh, praise God.* I thought I understood her directions, or at least a word in her directions. I grabbed a piece of paper from Todd, wrote *nombre*, and held it up to show her, checking my understanding of the word she said hysterically.

"*¡Sí, sí!*" She looked relieved and pointed to a line at the bottom of the check.

*Now I get it*, I thought. I picked up my pen and proudly signed all the checks with the word *nombre*, which means "name"—instead of just signing my name.

*Seriously?*

As a testimony to the fact he's God, he didn't look down on me and think, *I sent the wrong girl. She can't even cash a traveler's check.* He looked down on me and saw all the events of my life that led to this one and all the days yet to come. He knew he was leading us on a story only he could see in full, and he was asking us to step forward, recognizing we could see only in part.

Good thing I stand in a long line of people throughout history who are underqualified, ill-equipped, and unimpressive. It means that today when you see the organization we labor in transferring millions of dollars, pesos, rupees, and naira all over the world, you can give credit to only the Giver and not the carrier of good things. When people ask about strategy and vision casting, we smile inside. We have ways we could answer, and it can be tempting to try to spin it all so it seems sophisticated, but, in truth, the ministry started with a little girl hiding meat under her mattress, and I hope it hasn't changed much.

Ever since that summer day, we've lived and traveled all over the globe, loving God, each other, and orphans full-time. Some days it seems so glorious, and I am captivated by a God who I believe formed my story. Other days it's madness, and either my sin or someone else's has ruined me. When that happens, I want to be or do anything other than what I am in that moment. I gave up keeping a ledger a long time ago and can't honestly tell you which kind of day happens more often. The sun usually shines in my world, but I am sobered by stories and relationships characterized by more pain than is deserved. It was this soberness that drove me to *amen*. I hungered for the benefit of a life lived with eternal perspective.

My dad's early death rocked me. A runaway child broke my heart. A health diagnosis stopped me cold. The list of challenges grows yearly, but it was through these defining moments that I learned the hard way: faith does not make us immune from the chaos of the earth. I needed a faith defined not by result but by relationship. It fast became mission critical to learn how to hear from God.

## THE SPIRITUAL DISCIPLINE OF EMBRACE

It was the summer of 2015. By now, spiritual "shifting" had long become a regular exercise, and yet I still fought it. I made course corrections daily and had grown to enjoy the introspection required for a mature faith. According to my theology, God didn't cause what happened that summer. But he also won't waste any opportunity to speak, and I was in need of his next lesson for me: talk is cheap, people matter, and vulnerability is maturity.

My cousin, who was suffering from breast cancer, called from her home in Alaska to ask me a question. "Have you ever heard of BRCA2?"

*Maybe?* She went on to tell me it's an inherited genetic mutation that causes several types of cancer, including breast and ovarian and the type of cancer my father died of twenty years ago, multiple myeloma. She wanted me to know she was BRCA2 positive, and with my father's cancer history, I should consider getting tested. I was speaking a lot of words to her—I usually fill the conversational space when given the chance—but not saying much of substance. I didn't know what to say, or how I felt, or what to do, so I rambled on until it seemed appropriate to get off. I hung up the phone, mostly feeling empathy for her situation.

I thought later about our conversation, talked to a few friends about it, and considered making an appointment for myself. I waited in indecision, as we do when we are unsure, but later that fall, on a routine doctor's visit, I asked about genetic testing. Within an hour, they drew blood.

How many times have I been in a place where I don't know what is coming next? I sat there in the chair wrestling with *amen* in my heart. I wanted the peace this word offered, but there were questions and unknowns. *What now?* I tend to come to *amen* faster about what's already happened than what's yet to be. It was a familiar space. I've been here before. The questions have sounded like: *In which project should I engage? In which relationship should I invest? Is it better to go here or there? Wait or rush? Press in or hold back?* Uncertainty can pile up, and despite prayers, the answers aren't always clear. Led by Isaiah 30:21, I have asked God, "Before I take a step to the right or the left, which way should I go?" and been left confused by his response.

He's not being vague, as he is a communicative God. The issue isn't his willingness to speak or his clarity of message. The problem is while I am listening for his direction, he is saying far more than "left" or "right." He is speaking to me about my posture in relation to his and our connection. He cares more about our relationship than my life plan. He is working to root out that which is not sacred in me and create space for his deposit of good gifts. He has the long play in mind—transformation of a life from carnal to supernatural—and I have the short plan pressing on my soul: "What will this blood test reveal?" The competing agendas crash together and leave me weary.

In 1 Kings 19, the prophet Elijah was on the run and asked God to speak to him. This is the same guy who just days before had called down fire from heaven—and it came. The same guy who chased chariots and won. He knew God and had seen his power, yet he had this moment of self-doubt recorded in Scripture where he was asking for reassurance.

As Elijah cried out to the Lord, God directed him to "'go out and stand on the mountain, . . . for the LORD is about to pass by'" (v. 11). Elijah waited and a powerful wind came, shattering the rocks, but the Lord wasn't in the wind. I am sure Elijah was looking for him in the wind. It would have made sense, because the Hebrew word for "wind" and "spirit" is the same: *ruah*. If I were Elijah, I would have thrown up my hands (and maybe said with exasperation, "Can't you come to me in ways I expect?").

Then an earthquake came, but God wasn't in the earthquake. I have been frustrated before when I needed to hear from God on some issue and have asked him for the earth to literally move so I know he's there. But he isn't always in the big show, and I look for him in the big show more often than I want to admit. He is calling me to something deeper, while I am looking for something bigger (and missing him altogether.)

Then came a fire, and still the Lord wasn't there. I *always* want him to be in the fire. He has been a tongue of fire, a pillar of fire, a burning bush—I want him to come as I have known him to come before.

Finally, he appeared in the form of a "gentle whisper," or, as some translations write, a "still small voice" (v. 12). The Hebrew phrase we translate as "still small voice" or "gentle whisper" is *kol d'mama daka,* and it's used naturally two ways in Hebrew.

When a woman picks up her newborn baby and draws him to her face, making quiet sounds at him, the baby responds with his own inaudible communication. With her words, she might be meaning, "I can't believe you are here. I have longed for you. I love you." But she's using a different voice, and the words aren't all enunciated. The baby can't use language yet, but he's talking to her just the same. It's something akin to, "I need you. I love you. You're mine." Their communication might not make sense to anyone looking on, but for the two of them, in this posture of proximity and intimacy, much is being exchanged. Connection is being forged through these gentle whispers.

This is a *kol d' mama de kah.*

The other natural usage in Hebrew is when two lovers are in bed together, and they are murmuring to each other sounds only they understand, held together in a posture of proximity and intimacy.

This is a *kol d'mama daka.*

The Lord was expressing to Elijah that he is not always

found in the big demonstration: the fire, the earthquake, or the powerful wind. I will find him in this intimate exchange where his face is drawn close to mine and all others are now blurred out. This is where his voice is the clearest and where I'll be near enough to hear him address my heart's concerns.

That fall day, I sat in the chair of the doctor's office, and as the blood filled the vials, I listened for God's still small voice and felt his comfort come for me. It didn't have answers to my questions: *Will it be positive or negative? What will this mean? What should I do? Where have you been?* But something sweeter than answers flooded my being. *Amen.*

More than any other spiritual practice, what most prepared me for the season to come was drawing into a *kol d'mama daka*. This is where I heard who I was to him and what's true of me. It's where I asked all my questions and felt his rest. I am still a girl who appreciates a good fire, earthquake, and windstorm. They make great stories, and I love telling them. But sitting with Jesus in a position of intimacy and proximity has filled me with spiritual peace. This isn't peace as defined by the absence of conflict; it's more a sense of confidence, completeness, soundness. The deep breath it provides is his greatest gift to us, aside from salvation. It is our benefit from living amen. I draw in, and then as I deeply breathe his peace, the inevitable surrender—of my worries, plans, and future—follows.

It was December 23. I was dressed to speak at church that night, but the doctor's office had called me to come in for the results of the blood test. Eventually, late that afternoon, the doctor read the facts from a report generated by a genetics lab. "Positive for BRCA2 . . . 87 percent chance of developing breast cancer . . . 25–50 percent chance of ovarian cancer . . . pancreatic cancer, melanoma . . ."

The names and percentages started to run together. Images of my sick father, long forgotten, began to resurface uninvited. The conversation was pressing into a spiritual bruise that should have already healed. When my father died at age fifty-one, I brawled with God over this issue of when life hands you what you never wanted. The spiritual muscles under that bruise are now strong. I worked them out pretty well for a long season. I asked every version of the "Why?" question I could come up with, and each answer required heavy lifting.

I could still hear the doctor sharing this new diagnosis. I still trusted God. But it is conversations like this that remind me I might always be a little tender.

I found my voice. "And my choices?"

Chemoprevention, prophylactic surgery, hypervigilance.

That night I stood on the Christmas stage and told our church about the greatest story of all. I was aware of the congregation. I could see my own family sitting together, taking up a whole row. I shared meaningful eye contact with Todd, having not yet been able to privately process this with him. Publicly, I was holding a conversation about a manger, an angel, and some shepherds, while privately I was holding a conversation with Jesus about what this means, who I am, and who he can be.

I believe a *kol d' mama de kah* can happen both in private (a prayer closet or a shower) or in public (while the rest of the world is looking on). We can be in a crowd, a classroom, or the middle of a terrible conflict with someone, and God can pull us in so tight all else blurs but his face.

Once, when my son was four years old, he participated in a church choir performance. As he stepped onstage and saw everyone looking at him, he panicked and started to cry, frantically scanning the crowd for a familiar face. He couldn't find us and became increasingly upset. Finally, not being able to stand it any longer, I rushed to the bottom of the stage. He came barreling at me, burying his face in my shoulder. His crying stopped, his breathing slowed, and all was right again. He couldn't have cared less who was watching. He was desperate to touch base, and once he did, he felt safe. *Kol d'mama daka* has become for me a base touch. When I am looking out in the crowd, I see other people offering to comfort me, but there's only one face I am scanning for. I don't care who is looking; I need to know he's there.

Touching base in this way with the Lord affords us all kinds of his gifts. Sometimes it gives us peace, other times wisdom, self-control, patience, mercy. I have a friend who is separated from her husband. While everyone in her life is pleading with her to give up, she's tapping into a fresh reservoir of love for him. It doesn't make sense to those looking on, but as she shared her heart with me, I thought, *She's in a kol de mama d'kah with a merciful God, who is pouring his heart into hers.* We are capable of more than we allow in our lives, made possible only through extended time with Jesus.

When I received my diagnosis, I was in desperate need of the blurring of all else. Later, on Christmas evening, when everyone was strewn around the house, each with their new delights to entertain them, Todd gestured at the kids and said, "I don't want to do this without you. Whatever it takes, let's fight it."

## AMEN BRINGS PEACE INTO CHAOS

The next several weeks were hard. I avoided the subject and then got mad when we didn't talk about it. I read blogs, watched vlogs, scoured medical sites, and saw doctors. I learned how terrible the diagnosis was, and I educated myself with man's wisdom on the subject. As is usually the case, the more I listened to man, the heavier I felt. I took a nap every day, something previously reserved for Sundays. I decided to fast, hoping the combination of good health choices and spiritual discipline would make this reality suddenly untrue. I fought time alone with Jesus because with it came peace, and sometimes my human nature craved chaos. I was a hot mess.

I talked on the phone with a BRCA2 "previvor" and listened as she recounted her experiences and outlined the facts. To everyone else at the gym, I looked like someone enjoying working out to a good podcast, appearing thoughtful. I needed the information she was relaying, so I asked questions and quietly took in her insight. Then she said, "BRCA2 is like a runner gene. It makes cancer explode in your body, instead of stifling it."

With that, my knees buckled, and I fell off the treadmill. My mind was taking in her voice, but my body was telling me it was too much. There was a disconnect, and I knew the connective tissue of my mind and body was my spirit. It was time to work through this with Jesus.

The next day I sat down, opening my fourth Diet Coke of the afternoon, trying to stave off fatigue from yet another sleepless night. I meditated on Exodus 33:11, where it says Moses talked to God like one would a friend. I needed a friend. I started by thinking on what I knew to be true: God numbered my days. He is before all things, and in him all things hold together. God created me for all of eternity. And the more my mind sat in truth, the calmer I felt. This was going to be okay. Even if didn't end up okay, it would still be okay. I closed my eyes and prayed:

*Amen. You've always known this would be true of me. You have something in this for me.*

*Amen. I trust you with my future. If I do this well, I could be more like you in a year. That's a good thing.*

*Amen. I've seen hard stories and want to trust you in this, but I am afraid for my children. I'm just being honest. Take that fear from me.*

*Amen. What does this look like going forward? Only you know. So be it.*

On and on I confessed and claimed, "amen-ing" and "so-be-it-ing" until my heart rate matched my thoughts and my mind and body were in alignment with my heart. It turned out I didn't need answers (as I had thought). I needed peace. The word *peace* doesn't mean being laid-back or chill. The true meaning is close to being *settled*. Jesus and I talked face-to-face about this diagnosis until there was a sense of being settled.

When it came time to talk to others in my life about it, I used a passage in 2 Kings 6, where God gave supernatural fore-warning to his people of enemy plans. I said often in this season, "God is tipping me off to the enemy's offensive strategy, so I can play effective defense."

Now the king of Aram was at war with Israel. After conferring with his officers, he said, "I will set up my camp in such and such a place."

The man of God sent word to the king of Israel: "Beware of passing that place, because the Arameans are going down there." So the king of Israel checked on the place indicated by the man of God. Time and again Elisha warned the king, so that he was on his guard in such places.

This enraged the king of Aram. He summoned his

officers and demanded of them, "Tell me! Which of us is on the side of the king of Israel?"

"None of us, my lord the king," said one of his officers, "but Elisha, the prophet who is in Israel, tells the king of Israel the very words you speak in your bedroom." (vv. 8–12)

The next spring, I underwent a complete hysterectomy and a bilateral mastectomy and reconstruction. This has permanently changed my body, but I am not the sum of my parts. I am not "less than" today. In fact, by living well through this experience, I am now "more than." More generous, dependent, empathetic, and connected—and that's just for starters. The overwhelming emotion I experienced in this season was *grateful*. Amen has brought me to grateful. I felt grateful in the hospital for a private room and a wonderful surgeon. I felt grateful for heating pads, soft pajamas, good friends, the Holy Spirit, fresh flowers, genetic counselors, pain medication, peppermint tea, sparkling water, the Internet . . . and the list goes on. I honestly felt like my metaphorical basket was *so ridiculously full* that there wasn't time to miss or mourn what was taken from me.

Pain is a good teacher, and I was assigned to his class. There were days when conversations or side effects threatened my calm, but I reminded myself in those moments to draw into a *kol d' mama de kah*. I experienced a range of emotions I hadn't planned on having. I was mad at people I loved, who didn't meet needs of mine that weren't theirs to meet. I will always remember the people who took time out of their lives to come and sit with me. I will never say again, "I was thinking about you" to a friend going through something. I will put action to my words and pick up the phone, make the meal, or drive to her house. Jesus wasn't kidding when he said people will know who we are by our love. When someone loves you well, you are moved. This season, I was convicted about all the previous times I had put a task or an accomplishment above a relationship. If I am too busy for people, what exactly am I doing?

I sat more still in those months following the surgery than I ever had in my whole life. I talked to the Lord about subjects I preferred not to, and everything felt *deeper*. My love for Todd grew, my appreciation for our kids was profound, my thinking was complex, and my rest was substantial. I laughed harder, cried more often, and listened better, and I grew an appetite for gravitas. I decided I could skim the top of life, or I could plunge into the core of it and have richer relationships, including with Jesus. It was another defining moment, and it left me like that first one did: hungry for more.

In the most intimate of positions with him, we worked on my pain, and there I learned to focus on what was true. It is true there is chaos in a world God created otherwise. Chaos hits our lives, relationships, and bodies in all kinds of ways. This health diagnosis is chaos, but I don't have to stay there. I can shut out the enemy's desire to win again and again and tell him to go to hell with his doubt and mental attacks. I am building a platform of truth, each brick constructed with the understanding God's Word brings. As the platform grows, I have more than enough room to stand. I even have room to dance.

## AMEN GOES TO THE ROOT

Todd and I have given birth to three children, adopted four more, and long-term fostered another half dozen. I never imagined this would be our family, but now I wouldn't have it any other way. It means I don't have to go farther than my kitchen table for a field ripe with opportunities to grow. There have been thousands of moments when everything falls together and I delight in God's plan.

This was not one of those.

I was so over the fighting. I had been wrestling with one of my foster daughters over the subject of appropriate clothing choices. "Go back into your room and change out of that miniskirt," I told her. "You can't go to school like that . . ." She wasn't listening anymore. She had gone into her room and slammed the door. I knew what was next; we watched this channel yesterday. She'd emerge in something I had bought her. I'd smile and tell her she looked cute. She'd stomp out the door, walking to the bus, where I knew as soon as she turned the corner she'd duck behind the bush, pull off the clothes I approved, and reveal the micromini she had on underneath.

It was just one of many hills we were dying on.

Finally, I sought the counsel of a psychologist, who was visiting from Texas. He watched us for a day or two and then drew a picture of a tree, labeling it in three parts. "Beth," he started, "I want you to imagine the foliage of the tree as the attitudes and actions of your foster daughter. It's the part you see. Now, I want you to picture the trunk as her self-image. It's what feeds her attitude and actions. It has been built over many experiences and over a long period of time. Finally, I want you to see the roots of this tree as her understanding of truth, specifically God's truth."

I nodded. It seemed intuitive.

He continued, "The problem is every time you talk to her about her attitude and actions, it's like you're cutting off the top

of the tree. I don't know how much you understand horti-
culture, but every time you cut off the top of a tree, it just grows
back twice as strong.

"Her decision to dress inappropriately is directly linked to her
self-image. She doesn't see herself as having value. She is worth
something only when she is herself plus a short skirt. Your comments to her are like cutting off the top of the tree when what you
are really dealing with is a trunk issue. This trunk, or self-image,
is linked to her root system, which is embedded with significant
lies. The garden of her heart requires tending, and she must pull
out the lies. She's in need of an infusion of God's truth."

This was all making sense so far.

"Here's what I want you to do," he went on. "Spend the next
several months—how about we say three?—just focusing on the
roots. Fill your language with what's true about God. Tell her
what's true about her. Throughout the day, look for ways you can
reinforce what's real. Meanwhile, don't address her attitudes or
actions at all, unless she is going to hurt herself or someone else."

I had been tracking with him until this point. "At *all*?" I
managed to squeak out. "Not 'Did you do your homework?' or
'Get off the phone,' or 'Don't talk to your sister that way,' nothing about Internet usage, curfew, clothing, dishes, laundry, eye
rolling, *nothing*?"

I honestly wasn't sure I had it in me.

But desperation is a powerful motivator, and so as best as I
could, I spoke to her only in statements reflecting God's truths
for weeks on end. It was like I was speaking a foreign language.
I hate confessing it was harder than I wanted it to be.

She would come home telling me how someone provoked
her with a nasty comment at school, and I said, "Regardless if

they see it, you have incredible value and are wonderfully made."
She would complain about a homework project she swore was
just assigned that day. Instead of voicing my suspicions, I said,
"In him all things hold together." She would lament about how
everyone had spring break plans but her, and I whispered, "God
has big plans for you, full of hope."

My tongue practically bled.

However, something was clearly shifting. I started to
become more fluent in this language of truth and liked who I
was when I was around her. She didn't always look so poised to
strike when I approached, and I liked who she was around me.
She listened closer when I spoke, and her reactions slowed while
she processed my comments.

Sure enough, months into this new practice, she bent her
stubborn knee before Jesus and prayed her way into the kingdom. I remember looking over at Todd and whispering, "The
Rapture must be imminent, because *it is finished.*"

She and I are both still working out our faith with fear and
trembling. We now have a long history where we've proved over
and over again to the other that we care. There have been high
seasons and low ones, but I learned more about myself and Jesus
in those months than I have in any period with her since.

As I saw fruit born in her life through the process of root
pulling, I joined her by looking at the metaphorical garden of
my own heart and how the roots there fed my own self-image. I
would've rather looked at just her tree, but she wasn't a project;
she was iron scraping against my iron. I recognized in myself
that I had a tendency to judge my own intentions while I
pointed out and blamed others' actions. If I was going to take
living amen seriously, I needed to inventory what feeds my view

of self. Which lies cause me not to submit or surrender? Which experiences have caused me to wrestle for control? What hinders my growth in him?

A month or so after my foster daughter became my sister in Christ, I was making some New Year's resolutions, which tend to be false promises with shortsighted solutions. I told friends, family, our radio audience, and my social media networks about dreams to read more, eat less, rest regularly, and learn new skills. I couldn't help it. Every year, the idea of being remade into a better version tempts me. But the efforts are merely behavior modification tactics, and now I knew better.

One of these resolutions was to lose the ten pounds I had put on that year. As I was scheming my way to run more miles and consume fewer calories, I realized I was thinking about only controlling my attitude and actions (and, thus, cutting off the top of the tree). *Maybe*, I wondered, *there is a root involved in these ten pounds.*

Finally, after a long conversation with Jesus about my year with our foster daughter and all its struggles, I confessed a lie I discovered in my root system, one that was spoiling the fruit on my branches.

The lie sounded like, "Jesus had asked too much of me."

There was our big family, a large and growing ministry, a mounting set of responsibilities, and the demands felt, well . . . *demanding.* Because I couldn't sense *his* reward, I gave one to myself most nights in the form of a bowl of ice cream.

When I prayed about my load and whether he or I put it there, when I confessed how good it felt at times to carry something heavy, or how good it felt to take matters into my own hands, something supernatural happened. My confession loosened the soil. He pulled out the lie root from the metaphorical garden of my heart and planted the truths belonging there instead.

I can do all things through him who strengthens me. (Phil. 4:13 NRSV)

But those who trust in the LORD will find new strength. (Isa. 40:31 NLT)

All who listen to me will live in peace. (Prov. 1:33 NLT)

The responsibilities of my life were meant to be held lightly in his hands, not numbed by the chocolate ice cream held in mine. Getting rid of those ten pounds ended up being less about calories and more about confession.

## AMEN DRAWS YOU IN

In Revelation 2, God used John to challenge the church at Ephesus by saying, "Consider how far you have fallen! Repent and do the things you did at first" (v. 5). The word translated as "fallen" from Greek is used in other places in Scripture. It can denote a flower that has withered (James 1:11; 1 Pet. 1:24) or a ship out of control (Acts 27:17, 26). When I neglect spending extended time with the Lord, I feel like a withered flower or an out-of-control ship. A withered flower doesn't feel his peace, doesn't show his glory, and just seems tired. A ship out of control doesn't submit. It goes its own way, and you see it on the horizon, knowing its inevitable doom. Tired and out of control are default buttons when I am falling.

When John referred to the church's fall from the "things you did at first," he was referencing how the Ephesus church had once been so loving. When we read church history or even the letter to the Ephesians, we see a community so compelling that they loved both the slave *and* the slave owner into their church. They grew through community living and loving, but after their size was established, by the time the Revelation letter was delivered, their practices were a shadow of what God had once built in them.

How did they lose their way? Did they stop listening to Jesus? Did they do all the talking? Did they hear only what they wanted to hear?

Hearing from God in a *kol d' mama de kah* position can still leave a lot to interpretation. You might get an impression or a sense. The exchange often ends up being less about words and more about message. The message sounds like, *I love you. I made you. I see you. I forgive you. I will use you. Come into my presence. Go out into the world.* It's a spiritual language, and we'll spend a lifetime becoming fluent in it.

When I gave birth to my daughter Emma, we had been in Mexico for less than a year, and I spoke only rudimentary Spanish. The day I went into labor, we checked into a hospital, and a nurse came into my room an hour into the process, asking, "*¿Quieres oxotocina?*"

I had no idea what she was saying, but somewhere around the fourth try, I thought I heard the last part of the word, *tocino*, which I had learned meant "bacon." I looked confusingly at Todd. "I think she's offering me bacon. Must be a Mexican thing." I had heard my share of pregnancy tales—chili induces labor, and papaya curbs morning sickness—so I just assumed bacon was along those same lines.

He offered jokingly, "I think we should just say yes all day today."

I nodded at the nurse. "Okay, *sí*, I guess."

An hour or so later, by now anticipating the taste of bacon, which sounded oddly good in a pregnancy kind of way, I looked at her. "Are you going to bring me *mi tocino*?" I asked, sounding more demanding than I meant.

"Oh no, señora," she remarked. "You can't eat anything today."

I later learned she had offered me oxytocin, a labor-inducing drug, which I inadvertently agreed to. I met my daughter shortly after.

*Lots* can be lost in translation. I can agree to something I think the Lord has asked, only to find out later that I was mistaken. I then raise my fist at him, but the truth is that language acquisition is *my* part of the equation. He will always speak the same messages to me. He will always draw me in. *I love you. I see you. I made you. I forgive you. Come into my presence. Go out into the world.*

Living amen is drawing into this place where I quiet the rest of the noise in my life long enough to listen for this uniquely-for-me voice in which God is speaking. It starts with *so be it*. In the end, I surrender to him. The intoxicating presence of Jesus in a *kol d' mama de kah* is headier than a road map or a list of reasons why. So surrender ends up being less about off-loading relationships or responsibilities (which sounds like *I give up*) and more about seeing relationship with him as the highest goal (which sings a song like *I give in*). This keeps the ship from sailing its own course and ensures the flower stays beautifully in bloom. It's the kind of listening that guarantees love is our chief conversation and greatest aim. When I engage in this kind of intentional connection with him, each spiritual encounter has the potential to be a defining moment. Every conversation can look like an arrow, pointing me in a direction I had either previously not seen or purposefully avoided. The benefit of starting with amen is ultimately a release of control. For me, that release sounded like:

"Life can look differently and even be better than I planned."

"I have as much to learn as I have to teach."

"God uses struggle to produce strength."

And the list goes on; all of those lessons learned in the fire of a moment when my idea of good and God's idea of better crash into each other. I have a choice: draw in and be remade, or resist and fall apart. Is it even possible? Can this single word point my toe to the right road in the middle of any storm? *Amen. Where you lead, I will follow. Amen. I say yes. Amen. You've got me in this. Amen. There's something still to learn, so I'm in. Amen.*

# CHAPTER 3

# BREAKING UP
# FALLOW GROUND

## *The Restoration of Amen*

*Sow with a view to righteousness,*
*Reap in accordance with kindness;*
*Break up your fallow ground,*
*For it is time to seek the LORD*
*Until He comes to rain righteousness on you.*

—HOSEA 10:12 NASB

My friend and I hunted for a free table at McDonald's, eager to sit down and catch up on each other's lives. We'd started in the Starbucks next door, but it was loud and crowded. Over my friend's shoulder, I saw a pair of middle-aged men who were differently abled. They were talking to each other, often at the same time, and arranging a deck of cards over and over. The man facing me had dark, wrinkled skin and a nice, deep voice. It looked like a sweet connection for the two of them, their raised voices occasionally drifting to our table.

Suddenly, the man looked straight at me and said, "You. You, you, you, you, you. You need rest. You look tired."

Startled, I focused on him as we locked eyes.

"Yes, you. You, you, you, you. You need to stop. Rest. You. Yes, you." He gently rocked, not breaking eye contact.

*What?*

Just moments before, I'd joked with my friend about a speeding ticket I had received yesterday. "It seems the whole universe is conspiring to send me a message to slow down."

*Jesus, are you talking to me through this man? I don't look tired,* I prayed defensively. *I applied my makeup this morning, I am properly caffeinated, and I am alert in conversation. What does he see?*

"You. You. You," he continued relentlessly. "You need rest. You look tired. You. You. Yes, you."

I lost the last few moments of my friend's story.

*Okay! So be it. I hear you. I have taken over again. I keep forgetting to ask you first—about my time, my relationships, my plans. I am sorry. Is it really that obvious that it's on my face? It's time; I know it. I am holding on to too much, too tightly. I am working too much and on my own. Dear Jesus.*

"Are you tired? Worn out? Burned out on religion? Come to me. Get away with me and you'll recover your life. I'll show you how to take a real rest. Walk with me and work with me—watch how I do it. Learn the *unforced rhythms of grace.* I won't lay anything heavy or ill-fitting on you. Keep company with me and you'll learn to live freely and lightly." (Matt. 11:28–30 THE MESSAGE)

*Unforced rhythms of grace.* When I read that phrase, my soul takes a deep breath. I am a natural striver; I don't have to push everything through. I am a constant planner; God prefers rhythms, soft and natural. It's not about capacity; it's about tempo. I push myself to the nth degree, often to my own detriment. God offers unmerited favor, unearned and unwarranted. He says he won't lay anything heavy or ill-fitting on me. He says I can live *freely and lightly*. If our evangelistic pitches started here, how many more would listen?

Recently, I was buying a bathing suit and found myself in the dressing room with one I had no business picking up. *This must be what ill-fitting looks like*, I smirked, looking in the mirror. How often do I walk around in spiritual clothes that don't fit? Pretending to be who I am not or wanting something he isn't offering? It's never been his design that I put on what he was meant to carry.

Walking in amen, in the unforced rhythm of grace, is a daily conversation between God and me. It keeps me in company with him. It causes me to graft my moments with his will. *Which way will I let this conversation go? Which thoughts will I take captive or indulge? Which words will fly out of my mouth?* But amen offers more than just a personal spiritual boost. It creates shock waves of goodness in the lives of those around me. It puts the gospel on full display; it heals the brokenness within me and around me; it allows me to rest, even when all seems lost.

## THE BATTLE FOR AMEN

But will I grasp amen? The answer depends on which of the two forces battling for my life I give authority. One is the gospel, full of words like *redemption* and *reconciliation*. But our opposition has schemes of his own.

Instead of redemption, his plot is condemnation. He wants us to be lost.

Instead of reconciliation, he wants our relationships broken, for destruction to rule.

These oppositions can sprinkle themselves throughout my day and find their way into my relationships, affecting my attitude and the way I work. When I default there, aligning with the enemy's strategy instead of the gospel, I lose hope. I also lose my bearings, and I inevitably advance the agenda of the one who wants to kill, steal, and destroy me.

If *amen* had an opposite, it would be *no*. As I begin to fall apart and find I am losing heart, I can always track the start of the downward spiral to a *no*. (*No, that's not fair. No, I can do it myself. No, I won't admit that. No, no, no, no.*) Suddenly, I am defensive or overwhelmed. I am anxious or offended. I cut off the flow of the Spirit in me and insert my rights above all else. Turning any ugly moment around begins softly with an agreement to *so be it*. It's the subtle but powerful *yes* to lay down your life, to trust that his life being glorified is better than mine. *Yes, you have another way, Lord. Yes, I'll know it because it looks free and light.*

*Yes, I will surrender.*

## AMEN ANTICIPATES REDEMPTION

When faced with the enemy's plots—destruction, loss, conflict, chaos, decay—we can trust there is another plan unfolding. Instead of giving in to a disheartened response, we have a choice to join with Jesus, to surrender to a sovereign God who will make things right. My understanding of "right" has been tested and is still under development, but I picture myself thumbing my nose at the enemy—*You think you are winning, but it's impossible!*—when confronted with circumstances I abhor (broken relationships, broken bodies, miscommunications).

Amen waits for restoration and redemption to begin.

*Keep company with me,* I ask God throughout the day. *Write your best narratives into my life,* I plead.

I crave that chance meeting, the perfectly timed phone call, the check arriving just when I needed it. I want the *aha* moment, the you-did-it euphoria, the spiritual climax. I want to anticipate the gospel because I believe I was created for more than I allow in my life. Sometimes I lean into that movement, and it looks like maturation. Other times I resist, and it feels like war.

*Amen* is a word to be whispered throughout the day, a gateway to changing the spiritual climate around me. When I want to give in to road rage, lose myself in gluttony, or join in with gossip, this one word realigns me. It's an acknowledgment there's more going on than what I see with my eye, and in this spiritual climate, I side with Jesus.

I am drawn into God's agenda to make things new—sometimes with hands in the air in praise (*I surrender! Your ways are right! Amen!*), other times in desperation (*I am sinking. Come for me. Amen.*). God is not just making things new; he is bringing them back to where we started. He's always wanted more for me than road rage, gluttony, and gossip. So he calls me into conversation, and with one word, *amen,* my soul rests.

It was once all good. And his work in my life constantly reinstates Eden. He wants to connect with me the way he did with Adam and Eve before the apple. Am I willing to make room for connection with him?

When man fell and sin entered the world, God's intended relationship with him was severed. Only six chapters later, God reached out through Noah, starting over, reconnecting, and repopulating the earth.

When Noah used poor judgment, man fell again, and this next time God reached out through Abraham, making a covenant about relationship with his family.

Abraham and his descendants couldn't keep that covenant, and the relationship broke. The next time, God reached out to connect through Moses, rescuing this nation and restoring it to himself. He does not weary in doing good. He never stops wanting us, even when we fall. As he led the people through Moses to build a tabernacle, he made the same pledge to them that he does to us today. *If you make room for me, I will come and fill it* (Ex. 40:34).

Then man fell once more, and God reached out through David, showing us what a king after his own heart looks like. However, kings fail us, and so man lingered, waiting for a new way to connect. Their good and poor choices in this waiting season are chronicled through the stories of the Minor Prophets, and the whole earth waited for the return of a king.

Then God sent Jesus.

The waiting is over; my king has arrived. Now it's a daily decision on my part if he will rule my kingdom or if I will. His intentions and instructions have not changed. He still wants relationship with me, he still has a covenant with me, and he still asks if I'll make room for him so he can come and fill me up. Just like my spiritual forefathers, I must cling to the covenant. When I fail, my soul curls up at his feet, and I confess my selfishness, my pride, or whatever caused the fall, trusting he will be quick to honor that covenant.

## CONFESSION IS A JACKHAMMER

For years, Todd and I had a recurring conflict in our marriage. I don't know if others are more creative and diverse in their fighting, but we tended to clash about the same thing. It was so predictable that I could even tell you when it was going to happen: Saturday mornings.

We were living in Mexico, leading a large team of people committed to loving the fatherless. The work was rewarding but relentless. I would wake up and think, *Saturday morning is all ours.* It couldn't be claimed by the staff who were enjoying their own discretionary time, the orphans we lived alongside who were sleeping, or the guests still in transit coming to visit. It was at least a partial day of freedom for us.

I would wake up with visions of pancakes and hiking and board games.

*Bliss. Connection. Family time. Leisure.*

Todd would wake up on these same Saturday mornings, in the same bed, with our same life, and he would think, *Saturday morning is all ours.* Then his mind would flood with peaceful images of him rotating our tires, paying our taxes, and grocery shopping for our large family.

*Bliss. Tasks. Completion. Responsibility.*

I learned the hard way that another definition for *expectation* is "premeditated resentment." Our agendas would conflict, and, inevitably, we would sin against each other, sometimes in thoughts, most of the time in actions and words.

It was, as we call it in our marriage, a "disconnect."

In the beginning, heaven and earth were all living together in perfect peace (or *shalom* in Hebrew). Then the fall occurred, and the perfect peace of heaven separated from earth, now left in a state of chaos.

That chaos flourished throughout the Old Testament, and God, in his mercy, reached down over and over again to intervene and make things right, ultimately sending Jesus, the perfect shalom, into our disorder. Once Jesus ascended and left us with his Holy Spirit, he created a space called "the kingdom of heaven on earth," where the perfect peace of heaven rests full-time into the chaos of earth.

That's where my citizenship now lies. That's where I get to be married, raise children, work, and share life with others. This is where peace can rule. I am not yet in eternal shalom, but I have not been left to suffer in the chaos.

What does life look like in the kingdom of heaven on earth? It looks like a place where he doesn't put anything ill-fitting on you, where a gospel is lived out in reconciliation and restoration.

Had I been living amen on those Saturday mornings, I would have experienced more grace and peace, both needed to navigate those conversations. I would have been quicker to die to myself, to see Todd's needs as equal to mine, or, better yet, greater than mine. I had a spiritual birthright to be in the kingdom of heaven on earth, and instead I chose to enter into the chaos and bring someone I loved with me.

Hosea wrote in chapter 7, recording God's words about his people: "I long to redeem them but they speak about me falsely.

They do not cry out to me from their hearts but wail on their beds" (vv. 13–14).

That was me on Saturday mornings with Todd. I made a lot of noise and sent it heavenward, but it was a bit like running on a treadmill. I might've been sweating, but I hadn't gotten very far.

After months of this pattern, I came to him one weekend and confessed I knew I had been apologizing week after week, but I wasn't really sorry. I was feeling sorry for the consequences of my sin (the disconnect) and not actually for the sin I was committing (which boiled down to pride).

Confession is like a jackhammer. It breaks up fallow ground.

In Hosea 10:12, the prophet said, "Sow with a view to righteousness, reap in accordance with kindness; *break up your fallow ground,* for it is time to seek the LORD until He comes to rain righteousness on you" (NASB). Fallow ground is untilled, uncultivated, unused, or laid dormant, and while the phrase is typically used in conversations about farming, it perfectly described the part of my heart I had left to ruin.

I had believed I was the Queen of Saturday, and my plan was right. Sometimes I even believed it was holy. By messing with my Saturday, I drew the conclusion that Todd must be wrong. It wasn't about preference or schedule for me; it was about following my self-imposed laws. It was ugly, and it wasn't until I did the tough work of breaking up the ground through humble admission that I saw where hope could enter in.

Hosea continued in chapter 14 with wisdom for God's wayward people: "Take words with you and return to the LORD. Say to him: 'Forgive all our sins and receive us graciously'" (v. 2). I went to Todd, recognizing I had disrespected him, and took words with me, confessing the root of my sin and not just its fruit. Confession has brought both healing and an end to our Saturday morning fights.

## AMEN FIGHTS FOR RECONCILIATION

We are all wrecks, truth be told. Reconciling requires a basic admission of this fact. There is an ancient biblical practice I first learned about while in Israel called *sulha*, in which God, understanding how stubborn and prideful we can be, brings disparaging parts together.

A *sulha* is a meeting at the covenantal table of reconciliation in which two conflicting parties consume food or drink together. Once having done so, they symbolically announce, to each other and to everyone watching, there will be no grudge held against the other.

Usually when two people are in conflict, one person is the offender, and the victim waits until the offender apologizes for his behavior. Then they piece together a reconciliation that is usually an awkward exchange of "I'm sorry" with subtle guilt sprinkled in. Sometimes the person who did the wronging doesn't even know what he did. Suddenly, there is just tension and distance in a relationship. Or, occasionally, the one who did the hurting is busy damaging a long line of people, and that person isn't planning on fixing things with anyone. Whatever the reason for the brokenness, if circumstances are left to us, it rarely gets better.

*Sulha* flips the whole equation. The person who is wronged takes the *initiative* with the one who did the wronging, offering forgiveness and food or drink, thus symbolically announcing to the other and any witnesses that he now holds nothing against that person. There is no victim, no guilt, no waiting around for someone to come to his senses. Just a broken person acknowledging he has something to offer to the person who contributed to his pain. The sign of a good reconciliation is when the hurt person gives more to the offender than he is looking to receive. Beyond forgiveness, there is a spiritual space where the offended not only forgives the offender but blesses him. This requires a strength gained through a dozen whispered amens.

*You have forgiven me of all things. Amen. I learned this forgiveness from you, the endless source. Amen. You love them. Amen. Give me your love for them. Amen. You want freedom for me. Amen. Teach me to free them. Amen. You are working on them, so I don't have to. Amen. You see everything. Amen.* Each acknowledgment of truth releases strongholds and opens the window for God's spirit to come in.

*Sulha* is sprinkled throughout Scripture. Remember the story of Jacob? He was in love with a girl named Rachel, and to earn her hand, he worked seven years for her father, Laban. In the end, he was tricked and given the older, less desirable sister, having to work seven more years for whom he loved. The one who did wrong was Laban, and once they were all free to go, Laban chased after them. In Genesis 31, he caught up to Jacob on a hill. In this moment, I sense some good reality TV coming on. Jacob could have yelled at Laban, "You ruined my life! I don't even want half these people!" And had I been watching that channel, I might have cheered him on from my living room.

Instead, Jacob killed a calf, fed it to Laban, and freed him from any guilt associated with his actions. Jacob offered a *sulha* at the table of reconciliation. As a result, this grandfather kissed and blessed his daughters and grandchildren, and now the family was not defined any longer by what happened to them but was instead free to embrace what was still ahead.

That's what reconciliation does. It frees us to enjoy what is yet to come instead of robbing our emotional and mental energies rehashing what has already been.

We see *sulhas* in the story of Joseph, who gave his brothers grain, releasing them from the guilt they felt for selling him into slavery. We see a *sulha* in the story of the prodigal son, when the father rushed to the boy, then killed the fattened calf to announce to the whole community, "What this boy has done to me, I will hold against him no longer."

I think this was why Jesus was always eating with the tax collectors and sinners: he was busy freeing people everywhere he went.

We can read Peter's story of denying Christ three times. Instead of waiting for Peter to come to him and apologize, Jesus did reconciliation his way. He was the one wronged, yet he took the initiative with the one who did the wronging. Jesus brought Peter to the beach after the resurrection in John 21. It appeared as if Peter had quit the discipleship. In Mark 16:7, Scripture says, "Go, tell his disciples *and* Peter." Imagine how you would feel as Peter, recognizing that you failed the Savior in the most critical moment of your relationship. He must have felt like he was disqualified.

When we surrender, we give up not just what we have in our hands, but also what we have done. Living amen is a release of all things—both blessings we want to worship or take credit for and missteps that make us hang our head in shame. Jesus fed Peter a *sulha* of fish on that beach. He invited him into reconciliation, reinstating him in John 21 with an invitation to feed his sheep. Once Peter ate the fish from his hands, it was as if Jesus announced symbolically to him and the rest of the disciples who were watching, "What Peter has done against me, I will hold against him no longer." Not caught up in the momentary circumstance, God saw Peter's whole life at one time. He knew fifty days later Peter would be at Pentecost (as recorded in Acts 2), playing a major role in the church, leading ministry on a day when three thousand people would be added to the body of believers.

Reconciliation frees us for what's coming. It looks up and over the moment's indiscretion. It follows a way contrary to our nature.

This is why John wrote in Revelation 3:20, "Here I am! I stand at the door and knock. If anyone hears my voice and opens the door, I will come in and eat with that person, and they with me." Jesus is inviting *us* to the *sulha*. He fully understands we are the ones who have done wrong against him, and instead of waiting for us to get our acts together, he takes the initiative toward us. He wants to come and eat with us at this covenantal table of reconciliation.

It's a gift we will eternally enjoy, as the kingdom of heaven is depicted as a wedding feast (Matt. 22). I have had modern-day *sulhas* over cups of coffee and slices of pizza. Isaiah prophesies that when God invites us to the *sulha* one day, it will be a feast of rich foods:

> On this mountain the LORD Almighty will prepare
>     a feast of rich food for all peoples,
>   a banquet of aged wine—
>     the best of meats and the finest of wines.

On this mountain he will destroy
the shroud that enfolds all peoples,
the sheet that covers all nations;
he will swallow up death forever. (Isa. 25:6–8)

Reconciliations point to the ultimate victory, but that doesn't mean they'll be easy this side of heaven. I have been a part of *sulhas* where the enemy was dancing, already claiming victory over the death of a relationship. I had a dear friend, with whom I lived in community, who accused me of something I did not do. It was painful to watch one miscommunication and misperception spill into another, one misstep and misspoken word create a war in our minds and eventually in our friendship. It should have been the end of our long-enjoyed connection, but when we submit to the gospel, we submit to a process of repair and restoration. This is where amen collides with my sin nature. I need a deep breath so I can align myself with God's will. I need to bend a knee instead of raise a fist.

Starting a prayer in which I don't even know what to say is easiest when I open with *amen*. This little word opens up the space, and the spirit now has room to fill it. *Amen, she is your daughter and worth it. Amen, you understand what it means to be misunderstood. Amen, you forgive me for my sins. Amen, you are more than enough for what I need.* Amen stops a story from spiraling out of control and me from later looking at the damage and wondering, *How did we get here?*

I made a decision to move toward my friend, and she did in return. Today, our friendship couldn't be stronger, made that way as we demonstrated, through reconciliation, the *other one was worth it.* It's my favorite way to stick it to the enemy.

I cannot avoid circumstances when one of the many ways we hurt each other comes into play in a friendship: jealousy, gossip, impatience, and so on. However, in Jeremiah 2, the prophet warned of using our own thinking to fix it: "My people have committed two sins: They have forsaken me, the spring of living water, and have dug their own cisterns, broken cisterns that cannot hold water" (v. 13).

## CHOOSE THE LIVING WATER

We have a choice. We can fill our cups with living water and not demand from other people what they were never supposed to supply. Or we can go to broken cisterns, where water and thinking are poisoned and never enough. When Jesus is our supply, he offers plenty of grace and mercy and forgiveness. He *longs* to fill our cups. When our cups are full, we put him on display, and the whole world sees a piece of the kingdom of heaven. Amen.

The Last Supper occurred during the Feast of the Unleavened Bread. Leaven represented sin, so unleavened bread represented one who was coming without sin. In a seder supper, the head of the household would rip off one corner of the bread, called the *afikoman*, and hide it, symbolizing that one would come who is without sin (without leaven), hidden from our sight. If there were children at the table, they would be tasked with looking for the *afikoman* at the end of the meal and returning it to the head of the household. If there were no children, the head of the household would retrieve the *afikoman*, then break it into small pieces and share it with everyone who was gathered.

On the night of the Last Supper, Jesus picked up the

unleavened bread, and, following a pattern set long before that evening, he took the corner off the bread and held it up, announcing, "This is my body given for you [in essence: *I am the* afikoman, *the one you have been waiting for, the one without sin!*]; do this [breaking it into pieces and passing it around] in remembrance of me" (Luke 22:19).

Today, when I take communion, I recognize Jesus is offering me a *sulha*. I am the offender, and he is the one wronged, but instead of him waiting until I get my act together, he initiates with me. When I fill of his mercy and his grace, there is plenty to spill onto my relationships. He doesn't fill me with part love, part grace, part peace, part mercy, part patience, but with all love, all mercy, all grace, all kindness. When I find myself lacking those qualities, it's a direct result of the last time *I* met him at the covenantal table of reconciliation.

I can fail at this. I hold something against someone, either inside or outside of the body of Christ, and when I do, it makes no sense to the One who held nothing back to reconcile himself with me. Forgiving and initiating, loving and extending ourselves to one another, especially when the situation calls for the reverse, is the clearest way we have to demonstrate there is a God who rules our lives. This is a life that begins with and rests in amen.

## THE GOD OF AMEN COMES FOR US

We were gathered with our church family at a camp in the countryside of Mexico. I was holding our new son and watching our two toddlers playing in an enclosed tennis court, which, like a giant playpen, gave them freedom while offering me peace. Also with us were our two teenage girls, who were not enjoying themselves after the fourth hour and didn't hesitate to send me those nonverbal signals.

I turned my back to the tennis court for just a minute while changing a diaper, and when I turned around, my toddler son was gone.

Hurriedly handing off the baby, I ran to quiz Evan's sister Emma on his whereabouts, but at two years old, she didn't have much to offer. At first I looked around for him by myself, and five minutes later I involved Todd. At fifteen minutes, the whole church was searching for him, and Todd was thigh deep in nearby creek water, hoping to not find him there.

There are no words to express the terror you feel when you believe you've lost a child. We ran, cried, screamed, prayed, *hunted* for Evan for thirty minutes. I felt a desperation I'd never felt before and never want to feel again. Every sense was on high alert.

Then someone raced toward me, and I struggled to make my brain understand her Spanish, a second language I'd long since mastered. "*¡Lo encontramos!*"

*Oh, Jesus.*

My heart stilled. They'd found him. Evan had gone to the corner store with one of our teenage daughters, who, new to family life, hadn't realized she should let us know. They were happily sharing a sucker and walking down the lane when I ran to embrace them, kissing, swearing, praising, crying. *He was lost and now is found.*

"'For this is what the Sovereign LORD says: *I myself* will search for my sheep and look after them. As a shepherd looks after his scattered flock when he is with them, *so will I look after my sheep. I will rescue* them from all the places where they were scattered on a day of clouds and darkness. . . . *I will search* for the lost and bring back the strays. *I will bind up* the injured and strengthen the weak.'" (Ezek. 34:11–12, 16)

I love to imagine Jesus pursuing me the way I pursued Evan that afternoon. I do think he is on the hunt for us. He isn't hiding, as some imply; he hasn't delegated his search for us to an angel; and he isn't curious if he will find us (*I will rescue them*). He is undoing our lostness, both emotionally and geographically. He is cleaning up our injuries and returning us from where we've been scattered. This is his way, active and in control. This is what I surrender to, how I live amen. If I am scattered, I can be sure he's coming for me. If I panic because those I love are scattered, I can trust he is coming for them.

As a dim reflection of him, I love many injured sheep and lost strays. I don't have to wring my hands and wonder if they'll return or I'll make it back. I love only a fraction of how God loves them. If I want them back, how much more must he?

Saying amen surrenders to the promise he is on the job, even when his timeline doesn't always make sense.

Consider this example when restoration tarried. During the time when Moses went up Mount Sinai for the Ten Commandments, disgruntled people below were melting their gold and forming for themselves an idol. God saw what they were doing and burned with anger. He sent Moses to them.

When Moses approached the camp and saw the calf and the dancing, his anger burned and he threw the tablets out of his

60

hands, breaking them to pieces at the foot of the mountain. And he took the calf the people had made and burned it in the fire; then he ground it to powder, scattered it on the water and made the Israelites drink it.

He said to Aaron, "What did these people do to you, that you led them into such great sin?" . . .

Moses saw that the people were running wild and that Aaron had let them get out of control and so become a laughingstock to their enemies. So he stood at the entrance to the camp and said, "Whoever is for the LORD, come to me." And all the Levites rallied to him.

Then he said to them, "This is what the LORD, the God of Israel, says: 'Each man strap a sword to his side. Go back and forth through the camp from one end to the other, each killing his brother and friend and neighbor.'" The Levites did as Moses commanded, *and that day about three thousand of the people died.* (Ex. 32:19–21, 25–28)

The Lord's patience with man's choices ebbed and flowed its way through the next thirty-seven books of the Old Testament. The people obeyed and rebelled, and the Lord was gracious time and again but almost never more so than on the day of pentecost.

Acts 2 tells the story of Peter and the first church celebrating the Feast of Shavuot, as the Jewish people had for as long as their history could remind them. The tongues of fire rested on their heads; the Holy Spirit came to visit, never to leave again; and the church instantly grew. "Those who accepted his message were baptized, *and about three thousand were added to their number that day*" (v. 41).

Think that number is a coincidence? Absolutely not. We

love a God who has been redeeming what was lost since the days of Exodus. He gives back. He restores. He rebuilds and renews. He did it for his people that day, and he is doing it still.

God's plan hasn't changed. He won't lay anything ill-fitting on us.

He receives our confession as a fulfillment of his covenant.

He wants relationship restored and offered himself as a *sulha*.

He is relentlessly coming for us.

He will restore what has been broken.

We are not in charge of making things right. Amen.

We are in charge of confession and surrender. So be it.

Dear Jesus.

# CHAPTER 4

# SLEEPING
# WITH THE FROG

## *The Barriers to Amen*

*Moses said to Pharaoh, "I leave to you the
honor of setting the time for me to pray for
you and your officials and your people that
you and your houses may be rid of the frogs,
except for those that remain in the Nile."*

—EXODUS 8:9

I adored my first summer job, working on a roller coaster at
a local amusement park. They could have asked *me* for payment, and I would've agreed. Mostly, I loved my coworkers. It
was an early exposure to befriending people I hadn't grown up
with, and the diversity gave me a thrill.

I grew up in a Christian home and had long settled my mind about affairs of juvenile rebellion. I wasn't going to drink, smoke, or roll around in a backseat with boys, but I still had a tendency to live right on the edge of where I knew my parents drew their lines. Which was why I was frustrated when they told me I couldn't attend a party one of my coworkers was throwing after work one weekend. Didn't they know I was a good girl? No matter. I had my ways. Why they weren't suspicious when I told them I was going to spend the night at a friend's house *that same night* is a testimony to their good grace, but it left me free and clear to go to the party.

The amusement park was only a mile or two from my home, and although I was sixteen, I hadn't done much highway driving, so I arranged to follow a friend out to the party. Cincinnati, Ohio, sits on the Indiana border, but it still was a bit of a shock later that night to cross state lines and eventually land in Lawrenceburg, Indiana.

It didn't take me more than twenty minutes to realize this wasn't my scene. The gnawing in my stomach and the loneliness of not joining the revelry left me regretting my choices. It was too early to ask to follow someone home, so feigning bravery I didn't have, I told my host I wasn't feeling well and was going to head back. I vaguely recalled how to get from his house to the highway.

On the drive toward Cincinnati, there was a place where the highway split. Having never driven this far away, I relied more on the city names on the signs than the direction the roads were leading. One way led north to Columbus, Ohio, and that didn't seem right. The other way led south to Cincinnati, and that felt more familiar, so I took it. Turned out, as I crossed the

Kentucky state line, I was wrong. This night of deception was going from bad to worse, and three states later, I was lost.

This was before cell phones or GPS. My choices were extremely limited, and my prayers grew frantic. I made some crazy pleas to Jesus: "If you get me home, I promise . . ." But he had more for me this evening than a direct route home. Finally, realizing I couldn't get myself out of this mess, I fished around the car for a quarter, pulled over to a dark corner where the telephone booth was, and, taking a deep, humble breath, called home.

I started to cry when my father answered. "Dad, I'm lost. I'm sorry. I know you think I'm with Angie, but I'm not. I crossed the bridge and now am somewhere in Kentucky, and tonight I've been to Indiana and I know we live in Ohio and I don't know how to get back to you . . ."

God bless him. He answered calmly, "I'm glad you called me. Just tell me where you are, and I'll lead you home."

Recently my friend David told me he shares with his teenagers, "If you are ever in trouble with the law, find yourself experimenting with something you wish you hadn't, or are in the backseat with someone you have no business with, make me your first call. I don't care what you've done. Don't hide it from me. There is no one on this planet more vested in your life, your survival, and your well-being than me. I will fight for you and come for you like nobody else."

This is the heart of a father—and yet, in both the example of my dad and David, they are still just a dim reflection of the Father who stamped his nature in them. God is where that coming-for-you feeling originates. They are only a shadow of it.

On certain days, I find myself spiritually having traveled to three states on my way to doing things on my own, and I get lost. Eventually, I have to metaphorically pull over and humbly call my heavenly Father, who *always* answers with something like, "I'm glad you called me. Tell me where you are, and I'll lead you home."

For me, the fight comes between the decision to do the wrong thing and the realization I am lost. That conversation with myself needs to get shorter. It can consist of self-loathing (*Why am I here again?*), self-defense (*I deserve to make a mistake every once in a while*), self-righteousness (*I am better than the other girl; she's been lost a lot longer*), and self-pity (*I am always lost*). Whichever direction it goes, it's wholly focused on me. I can't get to a place of surrender until I acknowledge how my pride, fear, or whatever it is that tripped me up today got me here. Then when I throw it at the cross, it changes into a conversation about God, and I begin a journey back home.

Learning that strength starts with acknowledging weakness was such a surprise. I had the have-it-all-together routine pretty well rehearsed. In Colossians 1, Paul wrote,

> We pray that you'll have the strength to stick it out over the long haul—not the grim strength of gritting your teeth *but the glory-strength God gives*. It is strength that endures the unendurable and spills over into joy, thanking the Father who makes us strong enough to take part in everything bright and beautiful that he has for us. (vv. 11–12 THE MESSAGE)

I don't know which long haul Paul was referencing, but choosing to engage in a relationship with Jesus has taken me into story lines requiring glory-strength I can't muster on my own. When I find myself in over my head—short in supply on patience or wisdom, mercy or discernment, self-control or love—I cry out to him, "I am weak! I can't do it! Give me your glory-strength!"

Some weaknesses don't cost much to confess, but there's always that *one*. The one that feels better to hold on to, to nurse. It dances around my thoughts and feels like someone is tickling me. It falsely promises comfort and lies to me that it's no big deal. It is, or can be, my little secret.

Have one of those? It might be lust for another or a lack of forgiveness. Maybe it's jealousy, rage, gluttony, bitterness, or fear. Whatever it is, it's in the way. It doesn't just get in the way of life; it gets in the way of life with Jesus. The spiritual peace that comes from living amen, or the confidence I love to experience, can't fill a space occupied with something else.

## NOT ONE MORE NIGHT WITH THE FROGS

The book of Exodus records a scene in which Moses, the one God called to rescue his people from slavery, and Pharaoh, the evil ruler holding them captive, squared off with the plagues in the let-my-people-go story:

> Then the LORD said to Moses, "Go to Pharaoh and say to him, 'This is what the LORD says: Let my people go, so that they may worship me. If you refuse to let them go, I will send a plague of frogs on your whole country. The Nile will teem with frogs. They will come up into your palace and your bedroom and onto your bed, into the houses of your

officials and on your people, and into your ovens and kneading troughs. The frogs will come up on you and your people
and all your officials.'" (Ex. 8:1–4)

I want to imagine myself always on God's side, fighting for
him. But sometimes I choose to align myself with the enemy. It's
usually because I have a habit I don't want to break, a sin I refuse
to confess, or a grudge I would rather hold. Whatever it is, that
sin gets in my bed and into my palace. I find it in my oven and
in my kneading trough and on my people . . . Eventually, if I go
long enough without confessing, I can't see anything else, and
like the frog, it's everywhere. Then, like Pharaoh, choking on
my own poor choices, I must go to the One who has the power
to take it all away.

> Pharaoh summoned Moses and Aaron and said, "Pray to the
> LORD to take the frogs away from me and my people, and I
> will let your people go to offer sacrifices to the LORD."
>
> Moses said to Pharaoh, "I leave to you the honor of set-
> ting the time for me to pray for you and your officials and
> your people that you and your houses may be rid of the frogs,
> except for those that remain in the Nile." (vv. 8–9)

It was a stroke of genius on the part of Moses, inspired by
God, to put the ball back into Pharaoh's court. If these frogs
that had brought on utter chaos could be taken away, and the
one who put them there said Pharaoh could decide when they
leave, when do we imagine he would say for the frogs to go?

> "Tomorrow," Pharaoh said. (v. 10)

Tomorrow? Really? Not today? Not *now*? Pharaoh wanted one more night to sleep with his frogs?

And yet, I get it. It is wildly easier to complain about the frogs, to decide they are there as a result of someone *else's* choices, or to think my own solution for getting rid of them is simpler than confession. Or to think a few frogs won't hurt anyone, or maybe no one will notice because everyone is used to the frogs now. It takes work and confession and submission and surrender to say, "I don't want one more night with my frog." I am going to overcome fear. I am going to curb busyness. I am going to take captive those thoughts. I am going to forgive that person. I am going to be content with what I have. I am going to step out. I am going to speak up. I am going to take care of my business and then engage in his. Because if I don't, then my people and my bed, kneading trough, oven, and palace will become consumed with this frog to the point I can't see anything else. Dear Lord.

## AMEN IS KNOWN FOR LOVE

My friend Meme has become a sister to me. She was an orphan, then a widow, and she has lived in my home for more than a decade. Chronologically, she is ten years older than I am, but the first half of her life I count in dog years. It was a brutal start.

Meme was given away to a relative, who raised her as a slave. She has all the horrible memories you would associate with a life like hers. Promises made and constantly broken, a disregard for her wishes, a disrespect for her person. She walked from a violent childhood into a hard marriage too early but yet too late.

Decades after Meme staggered out of the home of her adoptive mother, the one who treated her like a slave, this woman reappeared. Now, she is very ill and demanding Meme take care of her.

As it all started to unfold, I confessed my lack of sympathy for the older woman. I know why she had nowhere else to turn. She was a terrible person who was lying in a bed of desperation by her own making. Throughout her life she treated people with disregard, and it was no surprise they had all turned their backs on her. What is it about us that holds a harder grudge against those who hurt our loved ones? Now, as a result of chronic and long-term illness, she had sores on her legs, and Meme would regularly clean them out and apply salve.

I suggested salt.

"If I hold something against her now," Meme humbly told me one afternoon, "how am I any better?" After I listed several ways I found her better, she went on to say, "And how, if I act unloving, can she see Christ in me, the very reason I *can* now love her?"

I agreed with her spiritual logic but continued to battle with disrespectful thoughts. Each battle represented a block in my heart to Holy Spirit communion. He said "love," and I said "withhold." He said "serve," and I said "punish." When I was self-righteous or judgmental, it felt good at first; sin can even energize initially. But over time, it wore me down until my thoughts and actions about this woman reflected a fallen world and not a redeemed one.

Then, one day, Meme's mother suddenly decided to change addresses, wanting to finish her life with another relative twelve hours away in Mexico City. She shamed Meme for not taking care of her the way she thought she should have, and I couldn't have been happier to see her go. I falsely assumed that when the circumstances changed, I would stop sinning. I agreed to transport her on the first leg of the trip, and so off we went on a rainy Saturday. Meme sat in the back with a woman so old and fragile, she looked like she might expire right there in my minivan.

I was quiet for the first part of our journey, not trusting my own voice. Meanwhile, Meme cooed sweet nothings at her, knowing she might not ever see her again, feeling as if it were her last chance to speak love over her. Meme recalled childhood memories (omitting pertinent details, in my opinion), comforting this woman with words of grace born from a heart truly redeemed. I internally tried to fight my own selfish nature. I knew my thoughts were not godly, and they started to feel like they were choking me. I remembered the verse in Psalm 22 that says that God inhabits the praises of his people (v. 3 ASV), so I turned on the radio to Christian music.

I was in need of some inhabiting.

We got lost, and no one but me seemed to care. I interrupted their conversation for the third time to ask Meme's mother if she recognized where we were. Did she know anything else that could help me find where we agreed to meet the next leg of this relay?

"I think it'll be near a gas station where you should pull over," the old woman offered.

*Not helpful*, I thought.

Meanwhile, Meme didn't seem to mind how long it was taking us to get there. She was using every last minute to free this woman from any obstacle standing between her and the cross. "*Mamita*, I forgive you. I understand all that's happened between us. I love you. I truly love you . . ." She spoke in soft tones, and while she intended it to be a comfort, it was like dissonance to me.

I whipped into the parking lot of a convenience store to ask for directions, and *crash!* I ran right into a parked semitrailer. It was raining, I had just wrecked my minivan, I hated how I was acting, and I was lost. It was like Jesus himself was standing in the 7-Eleven parking lot, hands on his hips, looking at me with an expression that read, "*Uncle?*"

At the terrible sound of crunching metal, the minivan went quiet. It was official. I now had a chance to demonstrate my faith.

I breathed deeply. *Jesus, this is where I end and you must begin.*

A teaching from Lois Tverberg filled my mind. Jeremiah 17 talks about two kinds of fruit, blessed and cursed. *Cursed* in Hebrew is the word *arur*, and central to this poem is a wordplay, referencing the Arar tree that grows in the wasteland. It has big, green, and full fruit that looks luscious from the outside. But when you open it, expecting to find juicy flesh, it makes a *pssst* sound, and the inside is empty and dry—just a ball of air. I've held one of those big, green fruits, what they call Sodom's apple, and was mesmerized by the difference between how wonderful the fruit looked hanging on the tree and how worthless it looked held open in my hands.

This is what the LORD says:

> "Cursed is the one who trusts in man,
>   *who draws strength from mere flesh*
>   and whose heart turns away from the LORD.
> That person will be like a bush in the wastelands;
>   they will not see prosperity when it comes." (vv. 5–6)

When I draw strength from my mere flesh, I run out pretty quickly (evidence found in my morning drive that day). There isn't enough Diet Coke in the world to give me what I need in situations like I found myself in the parking lot. I don't love people enough, I am not good enough, and I am not kind enough to treat someone on my own in a way that shows them Jesus. Maybe I can for a season or when they seemingly deserve it, but not over the long haul or when it really counts. That kind of love is a supernatural work that requires a supernatural source.

> "But blessed is the one who trusts in the LORD,
>> *whose confidence is in him.*
> They will be like a tree planted by the water
>> that sends out its roots by the stream.
> It does not fear when heat comes;
>> its leaves are always green. It has no worries in a year of
>>> drought
>>> and never fails to bear fruit." (vv. 7–8)

I stepped out of the minivan, surveying the damage. Assessing the physical wreck was much easier than facing the emotional one. I walked into the convenience store, a ball of anxiety and frustration. *When do I call Todd about our Mexican car insurance? Do I still try to get directions? Do I sit down and cry? Do I continue to fume and blame?*

I bought some water and decided to take a few minutes to cool down. As I drank most of the bottle, I literally imagined it as living water, filling my innards. It was a hot day, and I prayed as I felt the cold pass through me, *Jesus, wash me thoroughly from my iniquity.* A line from an old hymn floated in my thoughts. *Amen. The day is yours. The people are yours. Just help me, please? Dear Jesus . . .*

Washing of iniquity starts with confession. I had absorbed subtle lies at some point, passed on as truths by liars. I don't know who in our culture spoke them to me, but I know who authored them. They sounded like, *I am good. In fact, I am so good, I am better than her.* If someone could have read my thoughts on this day, they would have had all the proof they needed that I am not good. Another lie I had to confess was the thought, *We get what we deserve. She needs to pay the price for her poor choices.* I had displayed a bad attitude with Meme's mother all morning and felt justified in doing so.

Lies! These thoughts didn't have room in a mind bathing itself in prayer, so they surfaced, exposing themselves as destructive. As I said them, I saw how ugly they were, how damaging. I was not this woman's judge and jury. I was not better than anyone else. Confession brings reconnection, and reconnection brings peace. The barrier was gone, and I was back in the *kol d'mama daka.* I was ready for God's strength to fill me in this assignment. I had been called on this day to show a confused and hurting woman there was another way.

I walked back to the parking lot and circled the minivan, closing my eyes to the large dent on one side. I decided to be grateful I was literally stopped in my tracks. I called Todd and tried to share with him the giant spiritual lesson I learned over the itty-bitty van crunch we had just experienced (he still had a few spiritual lessons of his own to learn that day) and told him how privileged I was to co-mission with our friend.

After sliding into the driver's seat, I turned and looked at the ladies in the backseat, whose eyes were silently asking which version of Beth they would get in that moment.

"I definitely think we are lost." I paused dramatically. "But just geographically." Winking at Meme, I continued, "The truth is, in Christ we are always found. Why don't we tell your mama how he came and found each of us the first time?"

Meme practically giggled with delight. Her wingwoman was back.

It works so much better when I do things his way.

Amen.

## PRIDE IS OUR CHIEF BARRIER

One of my favorite ways to spend a free day in Mexico is exploring its natural beauty. Mountains, oceans, it doesn't matter; a beautiful place always reminds me of a beautiful creator.

A group of us were canyoneering one hot summer day. This is where you follow a river up and down a mountain range it has spent its life dividing. It involves jumps and climbs and makes for a spectacular adventure. We were about halfway through, and had hiked miles by this point, when our guide pointed out an optional jump. It looked like Pride Rock from *The Lion King*, all jutted out, practically daring us to mount it. It reached over the water, towering forty feet above. I was afraid. I took physics in high school, and I understood jumping off meant falling downward and going against my better judgment. I begged my better judgment to prevail.

Why I scrambled up there like an unthinking woman, I still have no idea. What I remember last before falling was slipping on a wet rock and rotating in the air until my feet flipped over my head and my back eventually smacked the water. From that high, it felt like concrete, and I recall my friend JJ crashing into the water first to get me. I was glad when he lifted my head to find the air so I could breathe. I thought, *So this is what the author of Proverbs meant when he penned, "Pride comes before the fall"* (16:18, author's paraphrase).

As I nursed a cracked rib or two, I had plenty of time over the next weeks to reflect on my decision to jump. I had overridden so much in my brain to make a choice like that. I suppressed thoughts of potential consequences, the image of my mother's face, understanding of my limitations . . . All so I could, what? Look good in front of others? Not miss out?

I wish I could blame the enemy for my poor choice, but the truth is, that honor falls directly on me. I get in my own way far more than any demon sticks his metaphorical foot out for me to trip on. I have a sense of self, and it's distorted. I think I can do more, be more, look better, sound better than is really possible. When I try to do it myself—whatever *it* is—overriding the Spirit check inside me, the consequences are tremendous. I often think what people need is more of me, my show, or my answers. Throughout all of history, God used love to grow us up. The chief barrier to love is pride. When I try to take credit or make myself, instead of God, look better in front of others, the whole story crumbles. Sometimes there are physical consequences; sometimes there are relational ones. But real growth and spiritual progress are hindered when self is put before God.

I had the chance to visit Bethsaida, a small fishing village in Israel, where many believe five of the twelve disciples hailed from. I had always imagined those disciple boys coming alongside Jesus, watching his godlike miracles, hearing his teachings, then traveling after his resurrection to Asia Minor and telling people who were godless about him. I was wrong.

They did all those things for sure, but when they arrived, they found the people of the Roman and Greek cultures perfectly happy with their own gods, who they believed healed and saved and provided. They had built temples to and hosted holiday festivals for these gods. What did the disciples have to offer these foreign cultures? Not more of themselves, not more tricks.

They had *love.*

Jesus had prepared them for this challenge. He told them they would be known by their love. He gave them great commandments and great commissions that were all about love. So immediately upon arrival, they began living their mission. I had falsely believed they somehow passed around flyers announcing "Service at 9:00 . . . Come learn about our God." They took the church to the people, instead of the people coming to a church. They loved the widow and the orphan. They reached out to the slave, the hungry, the sick. And as they lived out this God-is-love theology, people became curious about Jesus of Nazareth and his teachings. The house churches flourished as communities began to care for each other, sharing what they had and celebrating together, regardless of gender or class or color.

The church grew and grew and grew and grew until, four centuries later, they were the dominant faith in the region. Jesus' plan worked then and will work now. Why do we insist on bringing people to the church? When did we stop bringing church to the people?

We have to extend ourselves and, in that extension, give credit liberally to Jesus. The chief barrier to God's building great stories among our families and communities isn't our faith; it's our pride. He needs only a mustard seed of faith and will still do biblically sized story lines. He just asks that we always give him credit for what he's done.

The church in the fourth century became the cautionary tale demanding a closer look. Around the tipping point of the Christian faith dominance, they stopped loving and entering messes and going to the lost. Their pride caused judging, separating, demanding, and punishing, and, as a result, the church fell. In the absence of love and the presence of pride, the foundation cracked. Today, in that same region, where slave owners came to Christ and house churches offered refuge to sinners, Christ followers number less than 0.2 percent.[1]

# CHAPTER 5

# CLIMBING THE MOUNTAIN

## *The First Steps to Amen*

*Praise be to the LORD, the God of Israel,
from everlasting to everlasting.*

*Let all the people say, "Amen!"*

*Praise the LORD.*

—PSALM 106:48

Todd and I sat at dinner last night with a couple we've known ten years, and the man confessed his brokenness over a wayward child. We sat and listened, feeling compassion for them, wishing we had the right answers to immediately offer comfort. But a huge part of living amen is trusting God for the lives of people whose choices we can't control. It means talking to God more about them, but in prayers that sound less like pleading and more like resting. That's hard work and the antithesis of any pat answers I could've come up with on the spot. So we just listened.

Todd and I walked back home from dinner, talking about the kinds of situations that can tie us up in knots. I can feel panic over any number of subjects, some rational, some irrational. If I wring my hands over our country, the economy, my kids, or our future, to what end? I can't control the government. My choices are pray, vote, donate, influence. I can't control the economy. I can control only my own spending. I can't control my kids, leaving me only with the options to pray, model good choices, and love. I can't control my spouse, my boss, or my neighbor, but I can listen. I can intercede. I can offer. I can trust. How can we face a challenging situation and know how to spiritually navigate through it in a way that our souls stay intact?

The first step we've established is confession, asking, "Where am I living/thinking/loving wrong?" The next step is a release of expectations or, as we've defined it, "premeditated resentments."

And this is where it can get tricky.

Let me say the punch line to this story before it even begins: I am okay with it now.

It was a Saturday morning, and the only difference between it and a hundred other Saturdays like it was that we woke up in the United States. Usually, we were in our home in Mexico, but this particular weekend we were in the States for fund-raising efforts. We had left our foster daughters under the supervision of a caregiver. They had been in our lives since they were one and three years old and had been in our home since they were ten and twelve. At this point, they were sixteen and eighteen, and I loved them in a fierce way.

But fierce, I realized in hindsight, isn't synonymous with healthy.

One of them was difficult, always more work than the other, and, as the result of all that attention, the two of us shared an unusual bond. It sounds wonderful (at least the part about "unusual bond"), but, in truth, it had become destructive. She would come home in a good mood, and I would find myself happy. If she came home angry over whatever hit her wrong, I would emotionally wrap myself around her until no one felt the consequences of her actions except for me—including her.

On my best days, my intention was to protect the other children and my marriage from her volatility. On my worst days, I was okay only when she was, so I made it appear we were both okay more than we really were.

I wasn't fooling Todd, who was watching the tension build in our home. He and this foster daughter would war over curfew or laundry, and I would rush to get between them. Looking back, I am not even sure if I was protecting her from him or vice versa. Either way, it was a mess, and I was always putting myself right in the middle of it.

It was never clearer that things were not okay than during this short trip to the United States. The caregiver kept calling and complaining, and I wasn't there to get between them, so I begged her to be patient. Finally, she couldn't take it any longer and told us we needed to find another solution for her care while we were gone. I panicked. There was no one else left in our community who would care for them, every bridge long burned.

Todd called the house that Saturday morning, ready to draw

a line. He calmly told her she needed to find a friend's house where she could stay until we returned later in the week. He said actions had consequences, and she needed to experience them.

She roared.

She hadn't had to face consequences in a long time, because I had fallen on every grenade. I cried while she and Todd argued. I knew what I could do to stop it, but finally those actions seemed ridiculous even to me.

She moved out permanently by noon that day, taking her sixteen-year-old sister and all their belongings with them.

My world careened. I cried in the shower, I cried while running, and I cried in the car and at night. I couldn't hold a conversation for days while we wondered where they were. I faced the weight of all the chaos I had fostered in my own home, and I answered questions from my other children that revealed to me how dysfunctional she and I had become.

*How did I get here?*

The impetus was love. It always had been. I loved her, and, in the name of love, I justified behavior I now see as deplorable from both of us.

During the ground zero of this experience, I read over and over Psalm 91:1, my "9-1-1" verse: "Whoever dwells in the shelter of the Most High will rest in the shadow of the Almighty." *Shelter her, Lord. Put your shadow over her.* I begged him for protection and provision for both of them. After days of repeating this mantra over and over, I finally wore myself out. I stopped talking to the Lord when I went to him and just sat there, quietly numb.

That was when I heard him. He was speaking to my spirit in his quiet voice: *I have sheltered her since birth. I have always been her shelter; you have not. I used you there for a season, but your absence does not leave her unsheltered.*

Truth when spoken well and in love doesn't hurt. It heals. I could feel the tension release. Circumstances remained the same, but I breathed for the first time in days.

The girls' journey the following year was painful to watch. We reestablished contact within the first couple of weeks, but it was unsatisfying to get bites of a relationship I had literally gorged myself on before. I needed to relearn what it looked like to love and let go. They would come to the house or visit for a meal, and we would awkwardly exchange pleasantries until I would touch them. "How are you?" would come with tears and hugs and stiff backs and excuses. My cup would pour out, *I love you. I care about you. I want a relationship with you. I am sorry.* Sometimes we would part peacefully as they came home for a literal "touch base" and a sense they were from somewhere. Sometimes we would part violently, and I would cry out from the front door as they stormed off, *You are always welcome here.*

Surrendering to *so be it* hadn't asked this much of me in a long time. Over and over, Scripture promises peace in abundance, but God's idea of peace and my own idea of peace look different sometimes.

## AMEN SAYS YES

There is this funny exchange in Exodus 19 where God asked Moses to climb a mountain. At this point, Moses was eighty years old, and climbing six thousand feet would've been no small task. The Lord drew Moses up and told him to take a message down to his people, then come back up and share how it went.

If I were Moses, I might be thinking, *If I heard you tell me to come up, I could've heard you tell me what you want me to say from down at the base of the mountain. That way an entire day is not being "wasted" with the climb . . . And while we're at it, being as you are God, why don't you just watch how it goes down instead of making me come back up here and tell you about it?*

If Moses had thought that, you wouldn't know it, because he obeyed, arriving at the top of that mountain a second time: "So Moses brought their answer back to the LORD" (Ex. 19:8). How tired do you think an eighty-year-old man would be after climbing a combined eighteen thousand feet?

The Lord spoke to Moses once more: "Go down and bring Aaron up with you" (Ex. 19:24). He directed him to go down and get Aaron, then come back up another time! Again, if I were Moses, it wouldn't be hard to think, *Really? If I heard you tell me to come up the first time, I could have heard the direction to grab Aaron. Or, for that matter, why don't you just tell him yourself?* But we have no record of this kind of disrespect. Instead, we read of an obedient Moses who did just as he was instructed: "So Moses went down to the people" (Ex.19:25).

Imagine the stance of his heart and the conversations he would have had with God on his third time up the mountain. Moses would have been in a posture of submission. He would have been in a place of dependency. He might have even been begging God for strength, needing him for every step.

God had so much for Moses in that long week's walk: a lesson in learning to keep company with him, to listen for his direction. Moses learned to renew his strength in the Lord and to follow at all costs. As the Lord tested his obedience and subsequent submission, he prepared him for some big episodes ahead.

Just one chapter later, he'll receive the Ten Commandments. This was a leader who knew blessing followed obedience and consequence followed obstinacy.

Sometimes I selfishly want the big episode without the long climb. I want the proverbial Ten Commandment moment without jumping through hoops to get there. When I am thinking carnally, I see hoop jumping as inconvenient or uncomfortable. I want what I want, and I want it now. When I am thinking spiritually, I see hoop jumping as training, and I embrace it as an athlete preparing for a race.

Moses understood that relationship with God was about connection (*I am yours*) and not manipulation (*I do what you ask, and you do what I want*). In fact, my favorite time period in Moses' life to study is the forty years he spent waiting in Midian. He lived to be 120 years old, and his life easily divided into thirds. He spent his first forty years as Pharaoh's son, training to be a big deal in the eyes of the world. He spent his last forty years as God's instrument, leading and living as a big deal in the Lord's story. The forty years in between those two seasons were spent redefining what "big deal" really meant.

When we find ourselves in the Lord's waiting room or walking up a mountain for the third time, we can be sure he's redefining something in us we had all wrong. He doesn't waste a moment of our lives, even when we feel like we are waiting around for life to start.

I spent the first year my two foster daughters were gone traveling up and down the mountain at the Lord's direction. Going up and down again and again never made much sense to me at the time. I didn't feel strong. In fact, I felt weak. *I need you for every step, Lord.* But I was in a place where I had been listening to my own direction over his. I had taken paths of least resistance instead of the path of highest obedience, and there was plenty of collateral damage around me as a result. The year of metaphorical mountain climbing strengthened muscles in me that I still benefit from.

I enjoy my relationship with the girls today. They haven't lived under my roof since that Saturday when they moved out, but I still consider them family, and we have learned to live and love each other in healthier ways. It's not the ending I imagined, but the story's not over yet, and just as I have learned and relearned I am not their shelter, they have learned and relearned God is the only one who won't fail them.

## AMEN PROPS YOU UP

One Saturday, a friend and I were visiting a young girl who used to live with us. She was serving a sentence in our local penal system. She had wandered from our lives into the arms of a low-level drug dealer. During a routine drug bust when she wouldn't give him up, the police incarcerated her for the better part of the year, trying to force her to turn on his operation. Shortly after she started her sentence, she realized she was one month pregnant. So on this day, I came with creature comforts to make what was a hard situation a little more bearable.

We visited for the afternoon in her cell, and finally, it was time for us to go. I left her with messages of God's hand over her head and walked out, feeling confident I had been obedient by visiting her. Why does it still surprise me God is multifaceted?

He led me there to encourage her and to strengthen my empathy muscles. He also led me there for what would happen next.

To get out of the prison compound, you must pass through a series of gates and courtyards. During that process, I was "stuck" in an open yard with male prisoners and their visitors for about fifteen minutes. I just people watched—it was pretty ripe for that—and then I couldn't believe it. I recognized someone! I dashed over to the young man, who grew up in a children's home we had served. He'd given me a glass pitcher one year for Christmas, and I still use it. I had long loved him and was sad when he chose not to continue his education with us. I hadn't seen him in more than five years.

"Carlos! *¿Cómo estás?* I love seeing you! What are you doing here? Who are you visiting?" I asked, looking behind him.

His eyes filled with shame. "I am not here with anyone. I'm an inmate. I have another year or so left on my sentence." He looked up to see me flinch. "I was at the wrong place at the wrong time, with the wrong people." Studying me curiously, as if wondering whether I would believe him, he continued, "I don't have any visitors, but because of good behavior the guards allow me to walk around out here during Saturday visitation."

I enjoyed the rest of my visit with him, and we prayed together before I left.

I tried to see him one more time, but he had been released, and I lost track of him.

When Carlos came to mind, I mostly prayed he wouldn't feel like his history defined him, that labels like *orphan* and *ex-convict* wouldn't be the first thing people saw, but that instead they would appreciate his amazing heart, gentle eyes, and servant spirit.

As someone who is spiritually curious, I wonder about chance encounters like this. We seem to give God credit for them, but why? Was this serendipity? Fate? Coincidence? Something for him and not for me? Or a drawn-out lesson I would have to stay tuned for? I wouldn't get the answers for another season.

There is a teaching in John 15 often quoted about a vine and some branches: "I am the true vine, and my Father is the gardener. He cuts off every branch in me that bears no fruit, while every branch that does bear fruit he prunes so that it will be even more fruitful" (vv. 1–2).

John uses the Greek word *airó* when he talks about what happens to a branch that bears no fruit. In its lengthy definition, it can mean or be translated as either "picked up" *or* "cut off."

I spent a morning in a Turkish vineyard learning from Bible teacher Ray VanderLaan. It was like one John would have visited or had in his mind when he wrote about the vine and the branches. I knew practically nothing about this subject, so as we started to learn about working a vineyard, I took copious notes. A vine that lies on the ground gets a grayish fungus, and the fruit shrivels up like a raisin. Based on the passage in John, we would assume the vinedresser would cut off this vine. However, in practice, the vinedresser doesn't want to cut off that branch because it holds future earning potential for him. He wants to do everything he can to change its fruit from raisins into something he can use. So he takes a small wooden stake and props up the vine, with the hope that by being out of the moisture, it will receive sun and eventually learn to grow toward it.

Consider the other translation of *airó*. What if Jesus was saying that he will "pick up" every branch that doesn't bear fruit, instead of "cut off"? What if he notices us lying on the ground with our gray fungus and our shriveling fruit and, instead of waste, he sees potential? What if that moves in him a longing to lift us or prop us up?

We read in Greek the word *airó* many other times. It's the same word Matthew used when he wrote that the disciples "picked up" the extra baskets after the feeding of the five thousand (Matt. 14:20). The same word John used when he talked about picking up stones off the ground to stone Jesus (John 8:59). Or when Jesus told the lame man to "pick up your bed and walk" (John 5:8); or again in John 11:41, when it's recorded that Jesus "lifted up his eyes" (ESV).

In all these instances, this word is translated as "pick up" or "lift up," which is exactly the action of a vinedresser. If John was really trying to communicate a message of "cutting off" those branches, he could have used the Greek word *apairo*, which means "I lift off," or even *exairo*, which translates to "I take away." However, he chose a word that talks about his interest in the branch, not disdain. *This* is our Father: "A bruised reed he will not break, and a smoldering wick he will not snuff out" (Isa. 42:3). He is looking for weakness to strengthen and brokenness to heal. He sees what's ahead instead of what's already been.

It might be something we have to get straight one day in heaven with the Author. But just for a moment, imagine with me Jesus seeing our metaphorical little raisins or gray fungus evident in our marriages, parenting, or ministry and literally propping us up. To think he wants to prop up my unused gifts and unanswered callings makes me want to weep. We live in a world where we are so hard on ourselves and each other. Most days it seems easier to just lie on the ground and convince ourselves our fruit looks better than it really does or that fungus is in vogue. We can easily convince ourselves that it doesn't get better than it is right now, or worse yet, that at any minute the ax is coming for us and we'll be cut off. It's life altering to picture Jesus seeing our limp vines and, like a vinedresser who imagines future potential, propping us up, believing once we feel the sunshine, we'll grow toward it, and then things will change.

Sometimes our first faltering steps of living amen come with our hand in another's. This person can act like a stake, propping us up. The prophet Isaiah said it another way: "*Each one* will be like a shelter from the wind and a refuge from the storm, like streams of water in the desert and the shadow of a great rock in a thirsty land" (32:2). The Christian walk was not meant to be tried alone. It was always designed with community in mind. God commissioned us to go and share, so that one life would testify to another. This is how we are to work out our faith with fear and trembling. God wants to use us as stakes to hold up each other's vines, creating a holy place where someone can feel lifted up, sheltered, and shaded.

This is what I have to offer when I am faced with hard conversations like I had at the dinner with my hurting friends. I can't do anything about their son or his choices. I can't control how my friends are processing this challenging circumstance. I *can* prop them up as best I know until they feel sun again. I can offer them refreshment, shade, and shelter as I listen, pray, encourage, offer, and trust. It's not my job to figure out what happened and how I might fix it. It's just my job to care.

When I first decided to become a missionary, my mom gave

me a copy of a sheet she had kept from an evangelism workshop decades prior. It was a description of the steps someone might walk on their way to understanding the gospel. It was labeled -12, -11, -10, -9, -8, -7, -6, -5, -4, -3, -2, -1, then +1, +2, +3. Each number had a description of the attitude of a person toward the gospel. I think -12 read, "hates God, hates the church, hates Christians" and -8 said, "met a Christian who left a positive impression on them." Step -4 talked about how the person knew the basics of the gospel but didn't believe it was for him or her, and -1 was "wants to receive Christ but doesn't want to let something go." And then the plus numbers represented our growth and maturation in Christ.

It takes a whole church to be willing to meet people where they are. Some of you are great with -12ers and aren't intimidated by their questions or put off by their behaviors. Others leave great impressions of Jesus wherever they go. Still others know how to bring someone to decision, and they don't struggle with being bold in their faith. God has a plan for each of us, and we might just be a part of someone's story while they walk from -10 to -6. It isn't our responsibility to do anything other than love someone where they are and speak the truth unashamedly about how God has rescued us. When I think about holding someone's hand or staking up their limp vine, it seems to me that if we all spoke the truth more often and shared love more generously, we could be wildly effective vine stakes.

A couple of years after my prison visit, I crossed paths with Carlos again. The leadership of a local ministry to vulnerable children came to visit me, and Carlos walked in beside the man who had cared for him as a young child and who now leads the ministry. After we hugged and I asked questions about his life, Carlos told me he had returned to his mentor, struggling with the feeling he was a vine who deserved to be cut off. All he could see were his metaphorical puny raisins and gray fungus, and he figured it was what everyone noticed when they looked at him. It's a good thing his mentor had been given eyes to see as God does. He could have pointed out the circumstances that led to Carlos's arrest, distanced himself and his ministry from someone with this background, or shamed him into confessing his jailhouse actions. Instead, he acted as the wooden stake and propped him up, as God led, until the sunshine felt good and Carlos grew toward it on his own.

The first steps of amen are best taken in the presence of a caring friend whose chief ambition is not to change but to love.

Just like I wish you could lose weight without dieting or get good grades without studying, I wish spiritual strength came without long mountain climbs. It takes more discipline than I prefer to wake up, strap on my metaphorical boots, and decide to keep going. I have a hunch Moses had been climbing mountains a long time before he received the Ten Commandments. He was human, and those climbs had to have made his back hurt and given him a blister from time to time. It's just a part of the training. *Confess my sin.* Step. *Ask God what's next instead of making my own plans.* Step. *Sacrifice for someone around me.* Step. *Give him the glory instead of stealing it for myself.* Step. And on and on we climb. Like Moses, I have plenty of blisters from walking farther than was comfortable. Worth it? *Always.* When God sets us a table, the walk is always worth the meal.

The Lord has made us a covenant of salvation, one that spans the whole of eternity. He did not promise earthly comfort or freedom from pain. Demanding a pain-free life would be like a child who on his fifth birthday threw a fit at his parents for not gifting him a car. It wouldn't even make sense for them to give him a car. He couldn't drive a car, doesn't deserve a car, and wasn't promised a car. Why then would he demand one and pout if one was not delivered? I was not promised a body that wouldn't break down on this side of eternity. Why should I pout or complain when it does? I was not promised perfect relationships, so why do I raise my fist at the first sign of relational challenge? Isaiah taught in chapter 45,

> "I will go before you and make the rough places smooth;
> I will shatter the doors of bronze and cut through their iron
>     bars.
> I will give you the treasures of darkness
> And hidden wealth of secret places,
> So that you may know that it is I,
> The LORD, the God of Israel, who calls you by your name."
>     (vv. 2–3 NASB)

He has treasures for me, hidden wealth in secret places, and I want to go there and hear him call me by name. That's the covenant I can expect: God will give me treasures in secret places. There is friction when my natural attitude rubs against my spiritual nature, but that rub can cause maturation if I let it.

I have been studying Dr. Sandra Richter's work on the ancient idea of suzerain and vassal, the covenant relationship between a greater and a lesser party. It dates back to the garden, and the whole of the Old Testament can be viewed through this lens. These are funny words we don't use much in our everyday conversations, but the concept is easy to grasp. A suzerain is the master and holds the power, as well as the responsibility. The vassal is subject to the suzerain, but with her devotion comes the suzerain's protection. These are concepts that have been playing out in our earliest ancient communities and our latest junior high lunchrooms. Humans have been the same since the beginning: we want control. There are those who dominate and those who submit. My nature roars to be a suzerain.

However, as a Christ follower, I have handed over control, and now God is my suzerain, and I am his vassal. He gives the good gifts a suzerain does: a land to steward, protection from an enemy. As a vassal or lesser party, I am indebted to my suzerain, the greater party, and demonstrate my allegiance or faithfulness to him through my *hesed*, the Hebrew word meaning "unwavering loyalty" or "loving-kindness."

God gives *hesed* to us, an undeserving mercy to his people, and he asks for it back in return. It's how we say to each other,

*You are most important.*
*You are all that counts.*
*You are my all in all.*
*You have my heart.*

What's crazy in the God story is that our suzerain is saying to us the same thing he is asking of us. As a vassal, I must pay my suzerain a "tribute," a demonstrative gift indicating my willingness to submit to his authority. Most of the time throughout history, the tribute in a suzerain-vassal relationship is money, and when that money is withheld, it's a signal to the greater party that a revolt is forthcoming. When I decide to give tribute to any other god than the one true God, I announce my allegiance has shifted and revolt is on its way. He is looking for my tribute, not because he needs it or because it's a tax, but because he knows when I give him that which he deserves, I am stating my allegiance all over again. When we sell our souls and give allegiance or tribute to the gods of this earth, we reap the consequences.

My tribute can be financial at times. I pay my tithe, I give what I receive, and I am generous with what God has trusted me with. I try to hold stuff loosely, and when I do, it says to whomever is watching there is a God greater than my own wants.

However, my greatest demonstration of *hesed* isn't an economic token but my spiritual posture. It's an attitude that says whether I get what I pray for or not, my unwavering loyalty is to the almighty God, the One who has given me protection and a plot to steward. So I bow, trusting he has a plan, whatever I am going through at the moment is a part of it, and he is to be trusted in it. To withhold that tribute while standing defiantly is to invite unwanted consequences. The first step of amen is to establish who is the suzerain in this relationship and who is the vassal. As I bow my head, it's not just what I do when I pray. It's who I am before a holy Lord.

# CHAPTER 6

# SIN IS CROUCHING AT MY DOOR

## *The Challenge of Amen*

*Do you not know that you are a temple of God and that the Spirit of God dwells in you?*

—1 CORINTHIANS 3:16 NASB

Genesis is full of cautionary tales. We don't get very far in the Bible before learning what our human nature is capable of. In Genesis 4, God was talking to Cain, the second generation, when he said, "If you do well, will you not be accepted? And if you do not do well, sin is lurking at the door; its desire is for you, but you must master it" (v. 7 NRSV).

The sin crouching at my door is different from the sin at your door, but it waits for each of us just the same. If we don't master it—through confession, accountability, acceptance of his grace, life in good fellowship—then we have inevitable collateral damage.

If we are parents and we don't master our nature through submission to God, then damage is not only felt immediately, but also comes in the form of generational sin. This passing along of problems can plague a family line until no one remembers what it's like to live without struggle. One anxious person raises another until the third generation doesn't even know what it feels like to be free of it.

If we are friends, our crouching sin can make us manipulative, jealous, or aloof, and then what could've been community ends up being competition. "This is just who I am," says the offender in a friendship. "I get angry easily. Or I am judgmental. You have to accept me."

Crouching sin destroys relationships because within relationships we have the chance to demonstrate to a lost world God's stamp of otherworldliness. Fighting human nature is complicated enough. Add to it generational strongholds, and it can sometimes feel like a battle we wage with one arm tied behind our backs. This tie can be the bind generational sin puts us in. When we become self-aware and acknowledge where we've been ignorant of our weakness, change becomes possible. This goes a long way toward living amen. It's like seeing the potholes in the road and swerving to miss them. It's not easy or fair when we are trying to get from point A to point B on a road that needs repair, but this is the challenge of living amen.

In my own family, when I see my teenagers feel above the law behind the wheel, I know I have contributed to this problem. I regularly speed and have accepted as part of my identity behavior that is sinful. *I am a speed demon.* When I hear some-one teach about how generational sin falls on what I imagine as an innocent next generation, I get frustrated with this spiritual law. Shouldn't their own problems be enough? Why do they have to deal with mine too? Working with orphans, I find it madly unfair that some children have to pay an even heavier price for being the offspring of someone who has not only left them but left them with spiritual baggage. How do we master this crouching sin at the door?

Look at my example of reckless driving. When my daughter Emma got into her first fender bender, it wasn't God's being unfair—*she's the product of a reckless driver, so she must be a reckless driver*—but more the natural consequence of being around someone whose life is characterized by this sin. She didn't have reinforced traffic safety growing up. Watching me, she probably learned you just don't want to get caught.

The Bible gives us a clear example of what happens when sin goes unchecked in a family line. Despite God's warning, Cain ended up not mastering what was behind his door, and in his anger he killed his brother Abel. Several generations later, Cain's great-great-great grandson was a man named Lamech and it seems his struggles were a lot like Cain's.

In Genesis 4:23–24, Lamech said, "I have killed a man for wounding me; and a boy for striking me; If Cain is avenged sevenfold, Then Lamech seventy-sevenfold" (NASB).

It would appear anger management was never addressed in this family line. One angry man trained up another and another, leaving behind a trail of consequences and at least a couple of recorded murders. Which is why I think Jesus later directly ref-erenced this passage by imploring his people to forgive seventy times seven. In essence, he said if the sons of man are thirsty for vengeance seventy times seven, then the sons of light will be thirsty for forgiveness by the same measure.

Contrast this story of an angry Lamech with Noah. Noah was the great-grandson of Enoch, and we read in Genesis 5:24 of his legacy: "Enoch walked faithfully with God." It was his strength of character and unwavering faith that was passed down to his great-grandson Noah, the man who built the ark and saved the world.

How many of us can name our eight great-grandparents off the top of our heads? I was raised in a future-oriented culture that spends more time looking ahead than considering the lessons learned from the past. However, this biblical Hebrew culture knew their geneology, and we can bet Lamech was familiar with Cain's name and Noah with Enoch's. Their stories, and the manner in which they were shared, significantly influenced each of these men, one to take vengeance and the other to have great faith.

Still in Genesis, we read of Nimrod, Noah's great-grandson. He was a mighty, heroic warrior, a great hunter in the Lord's sight. However, discontent to rule over only his own house, he was driven to build the empire from which Babel and the whole empire of Babylonia was born.

What is so interesting about Nimrod's story is that he was the son of Cush and grandson of Ham. Ham was the one son who had the opportunity to protect his dad, Noah, when he got drunk and naked. Instead, Ham used the moment to ridicule and exploit him. Noah's response was to curse another of Ham's sons, calling Canaan a servant among servants. Canaan, the new family black sheep, was Nimrod's uncle, and the story of his choices inevitably would have been whispered among the family. You can believe Nimrod heard of it his whole life. He heard his father's warning: don't be a weak servant like my brother; be strong and make a name for yourself and this family.

Many people think Nimrod was the architect of the Tower of Babel. His drive to rule the sons of Noah somewhere turned evil in intent, and he forgot to submit his plans to the Lord. As a result, we now have more tongues than we can count, a protection our Father placed to prevent another attempt by man to rule the whole world. Sin crouching, left unchecked, doesn't affect only our lives in isolation. It takes down families, ruins friendships, and splits churches. The bravest acts I've done as a Christ follower have been facing and addressing sin I'd rather ignore. The most heroic Christians aren't the ones busy building kingdoms in the form of large churches and impressive ministries. The most heroic Christians are real people who have gotten real honest about their real issues. I want to sit with them for hours on end, listening to their tales of recovery and regrowth and rebuilding.

We have so many factors entering into our personhood: birth order, temperament, culture, education, gender, personality, and family influence, just to name a few. It would be easy to point to any of these areas and decide living with sin is an inevitable result of growing up in *this* family, being a middle child, having a strong personality . . . It's Satan's song he sings over us: "Nothing can or will change. This is simply who you are. This is what you get." The lie couldn't get any stauncher, and the stakes from breaking free couldn't be any higher. There is very little in life we really have control over, and this is pretty much it: I control whose voice I listen to and what I do with my soul. Might as well make the most of it.

## AMEN MAKES ANOTHER WAY

There is another way. Every single time we put to death our natural selves and tap into our spiritual selves, we put God on display. Hear that clearly: *every single time we put to death our natural selves and tap into our spiritual selves, we put God on display.*

Throughout Scripture, God calls us to be his priests. 1 Peter 2:9 says, "You are . . . a royal priesthood." That means our chief concern in every interaction should be to show others what God is like. That's the why behind meeting human need: to give someone a picture of what God is like. When I am acting like his priest, next to you acting like his priest, then together we make up a kingdom of priests. It's a stunning demonstration to a world used to watching people fall apart instead of come together.

I am a fan of NASCAR racing, and I have had a chance to watch a pit crew up close. These people with a specific skill set synchronize to meet the needs of the car when it comes into the pit. Everyone has only a few seconds to touch the car and do his work. Then as it races away, the crew cheers the car on, hoping what they did will make a difference. God has clearly asked us to be in each other's pit crews, to cheer each other on while playing a specific role and hoping our little few seconds of hands-on time helped. I am breathless at who is in my pit crew and all the ways they have filled me up. Why does he tell us so often to enter into each other's lives? So that through each other, we would see *him* for a moment.

It's a challenge to consider this biblical truth of putting God on display when I enter into conflict and would prefer to show someone I am right rather than who God is. Or, in all honesty, I don't need people to know I am right, as long as they know how wrong they are. When I am meeting others' needs, it's hard to have a clear conscience that my only motivation is their understanding of God and not their opinion of me.

Being a priest means I am more than the *recipient* of his goodness, mercy, forgiveness, gifts, and grace. Being a priest means I am a *conduit* of his goodness, mercy, forgiveness, gifts, and grace. This conduit comes from the regular practice of putting my own needs last. I am deeply tested by this, as I want to naturally go first in line and make myself the most comfortable. I have to put that natural self to death in order for someone to see the supernatural at work in me and then wonder less about Beth and more about Jesus.

It means less show, more substance. Wouldn't this be a lovely world to live in?

Back2Back, the organization Todd and I work for, had been laboring to construct a second floor on a church in a marginalized community for at least two years. The progress was steady but *slow*. Our deal with the pastor, José Ángel, was we would provide the materials if he and the men in his community would provide the labor. The project had been inching along for a while when I learned one of the donors would be coming for a visit in a few months. I was hoping we could have the ribbon cutting when he arrived.

I approached the pastor. "I know you have been working hard, and I love all that has happened so far. How about I come up with extra funds to help pay for additional labor?"

José Ángel looked at me skeptically.

I forged on. "Then you can see this project finished in the next month or so." I beamed, thinking how grateful he would be at this generous offer.

Imagine my surprise when he answered, "*No gracias.* I don't want more money, and I don't want more laborers. If you try to finish this floor, I will secretly come in at night and undo it. If it gets finished, even though I don't need it quite yet, I will start a third floor." He fixed his gaze on me and didn't blink.

I could see I was being challenged, but why? "I thought you would be happy." I tried not to sound defensive.

"I couldn't ever get the men in this community to come out to a Bible study or a men's group, but someone will come out to work on this building each day. Men show up all throughout the week. When they go to a job site and there isn't work available, they'll come on over here. By putting in a day's worth of work, they can go home dirty. Their families see them as working, and there is dignity in that. On Saturdays and Sundays, we have a crowd here working. They are afraid of Bible study. They aren't afraid of construction. This is my discipleship program. Don't go messing with that."

As realization dawned, I dropped my head in confession. It was time to put the natural self to death—the one that wanted to complete the project and get the pat on the head and feel like we had something to *show* for our work. I hadn't been looking with kingdom eyes, but once I did, I realized José Ángel was right. While I was valuing completion, accomplishment, the show of it all, he was valuing relationship, personal dignity, and coming alongside of it all. The sins crouching at my door—pride, self-importance, success—had mastered me. But I am a work in progress, and God promises he isn't finished with me yet. So, taking a deep breath, I did the hard thing in order to experience the good later and said, "I am sorry, José Ángel. You are right." (Always the right way to start.) "What can I do?"

In Galatians 6:2, Paul wrote, "Carry each other's burdens, and in this way you will fulfill the law of Christ." A few verses later, though, he instructed, "Each one should carry their own load" (v. 5). So, Apostle Paul, which one is it? Should we carry someone's burden or let people carry their own loads?

In the original language, a "load" is referred to as the weight of a soldier's backpack, around thirty-five pounds. Paul is teaching us it's good and right to carry our own backpacks, something manageable for one person. This is the work God has for us, the curse of the original fall, and the cost of living on the earth. This is what the men were picking up each day when they came to the church in their community to work. We need to not only carry our backpacks but also allow others to carry their own. To take on other people's weight robs them of their dignity and creates the victim mentality we can easily perpetuate in well-intentioned yet poorly executed social justice.

However, Paul equally teaches that someone else's burden is our privilege to share. It's more than what we can do on our own. The discernment required to differentiate between load and burden is critical. The first step is asking where my natural way is dominating my spiritual nature. How are my own ideas interfering with God's spiritual principles? Where is my sin hindering this relationship or project?

I tried to pick up José Ángel's backpack, and, worse yet, I did it so I could look better. I saw a finished project as the highest goal and was reminded once again that in God's economy, relationship is king. Crouching at my door was the sin of pride. Once I was confronted with my sin, I had a choice. I could die to self, which meant choosing God's way, listening to wisdom, and loving others chiefly, or I could cave to sin. When I chose love, I put to death my sinful nature and shut the door on sin. Now the men in the community, the pastors, the donors, and all of us who have worshipped there see what God, not man, has built. Imagine how much of his glory I would have robbed if I'd insisted on my own way.

A prayer that starts with *amen* lets go. It pivots and feels conviction and makes course corrections. It's an eager student and doesn't care who gets credit. Its highest goal is to put God on display.

## AMEN BRINGS THE CHURCH TOGETHER

It's one thing to be a priest all alone and quite another to do so in community with others. The body of Christ working together is the principal avenue we have to demonstrate God's way really works. 1 Corinthians 3:16 says, "Do you not know that *you* [which is in the plural form, like *you all*] are a *temple* [singular] of God and that the Spirit of God dwells in you?" (NASB). We make up his one body all together, announcing to the world that God is so real it doesn't matter if we are wildly different and completely broken. We can still love each other like family.

It's within this body of Christ that we can transform and break generational sin. We first call it out in each other, and that takes real courage. It says, "Your holiness is important to me." Then we have to pray for each other. This says, "Your holiness is worth my time and effort." Finally, we have to hold one another accountable as God's new work in us takes root. This says, "Your holiness is of more value to me than my comfort."

It's in this kind of community where I cultivate an appetite for conversations of substance that leave me challenged to sacrifice more, listen better, and be set apart. These relationships will be under attack by an enemy who prefers us divided, and they require more work than our technology-driven culture often asks of us. When the church acts like it should, it feels like a family reunion, a place we are known.

## FAMILIES STICK TOGETHER

Years ago, we took in a fourteen-year-old girl named Olga. She was well behaved, kept to herself, did her laundry, came to dinner on time, and finished her homework. For a while, she made me think either *This is easy* or *I am good*. Then, as trauma does, it rears its head when the vessel feels safest. Within six months, Olga started a downward trend. First she cut off her hair, then dressed in all black, then changed her music station and viewing choices. These were all external signs her shift was linked to an internal battle.

"It's time for dinner, Olga," I'd say.

"Why do you get so defensive when I don't want to eat what you prepare?" She wasted no time in drawing her sword.

"We'd love your company at the table." I tried to be the bigger person, but I confess to not always feeling it.

Black fingernail polish, regular scowling, a new group of friends, plummeting grades—it didn't take a lot to notice we were heading for a cliff.

Every time I took this relationship to the Lord, he answered the same. *Love her, Beth. Love her rolling eyes and clamped-up mouth. Love her as I do.*

Olga's crouching sin had to do with her extreme I-don't-need-anyone belief. She didn't want me to pray with her anymore, so Todd and I took to laying hands on the exterior walls of our home, right outside her bedroom. We prayed loudly for the Savior to come, realizing he had long been involved. We asked for protection, breakthrough, forgiveness. I whispered—usually loud enough for just me and Jesus to hear—"Give me love for her, Lord."

Olga was not a dramatic girl; she tried to stay under the radar in every conceivable way. So it shouldn't surprise me that she walked out of this phase as quietly as possible. I noticed small signs of hope. She lingered at the dinner table and lifted her head in acknowledgment when she entered the house. I started to call her Lucecita, which means "little light." It was my signal to her that I saw it. Her style wasn't ever going to be a blinding spotlight, but the candle flicker was enough for me.

She spent the next eight years being friendly, occasionally supportive, and in general, compliant, but there was still some distance. As she grew, she lived off and on with us throughout college, and she was still very independent, but not in a good way. Olga got a job we didn't know about to buy glasses for herself we didn't know she needed. Instead of planning for her graduation together, we were informed of her plans. I had created my own set of expectations for her, and, I suppose, she had for me. We had settled into a nice, amicable, steady relationship. But I always wanted more.

We moved back to the States when Olga was twenty-five. She said good-bye to us but without many tears.

"I'll have a plane ticket for you anytime you want one," I said to her, holding her face in my hands. She made many excuses not to visit us—the weather, her job, bad timing. I wondered if we'd ever get the chance to love on her again.

I traveled to Mexico for her birthday last year and brought her some packages. She finished opening them and was wildly enthusiastic, very out of character. "I *love* these shoes. This book looks *terrific*! This jacket is *just* what I need . . ."

Something was clearly up.

"What are you all doing for Christmas this year?" Olga asked as casually as she could muster.

"I think we'll be in Ohio," I said tentatively and slowly. *Where is she going with this?*

"I was wondering"—she looked down—"if I could come home this year."

"Home? With us? Of course!" I said. First of all, she had never considered Ohio her home, and secondly, she had never asked to be with us. I couldn't help myself. Instead of riding the wave I had just caught, I had to know. "What is up? Tell me. You love my gifts, and now you want to come home this Christmas?"

Olga smirked. (There she was.) "I've been seeing a counselor, and he told me I need to do a better job asking for what I want from those I love."

She had me at "those I love."

I was now putty in her hands and practically jumped on her lap. I gushed, "Of course you can come home."

She smiled back at me sheepishly, seeming very proud of herself.

I made the ticket for a five-day visit, thinking I might as well not push it. Better to leave her with a good impression rather than a full-court press. The visit over Christmas went well, and the night before she left, I was sitting on her suitcase, helping her close up all the swag she had gathered on her trip. Olga was stalling during the packing process. Finally, I met her eyes and squinted. *What are you thinking?* my familiar look implied.

"I am not ready to leave." I knew this admission cost her something and was evidence of the sin at her door she was fighting to master.

"I was never ready for you to go," I confessed.

She held my gaze, wondering if I was talking about today or yesterday.

I stood to hug her. "So, that's settled. Let's go change your ticket."

She hugged me back. (I hear fireworks somewhere.)

"I love you."

*"Lo sé. Yo también te amo."*

I know? (*¿Yo sé?*) Isn't that the holy grail of loving—not that we are just expressing but the recipient is receiving? She knows she is loved. Is there any greater gift we can give another? Is this how we support each other as we all face the sin at our own doors? Is it possible love is what gives us courage, holds our hands, and fights alongside us? Then why are we all so busy offering advice, enlisting in programs, and beating ourselves back into submission? Love makes us family, and family sticks together. I will grow up alongside you while you grow up alongside me. And miraculously, as I stick with you and believe for you, God will use that to mature me too.

I was talking to a pastor I had met just fifteen minutes prior. We were backstage on a Sunday morning, and I was a guest speaker at his church. We chatted about missions, his children, and common friends until it was time for us to go in front of the congregation. He prayed for me, and I waited while he went first to greet everyone and introduce me.

The pastor went through the normal details, then said, "And so, everyone, let's welcome home *our* missionary Beth Guckenberger."

I walked onstage smiling but shot him a confused look. I hoped it said, *I am not your missionary, and this is not where I should be welcomed home. We both know I just met you, but if you want to sell them some story about my being from here, I won't out you.*

He plainly read my face because he smiled and turned toward the congregation. "Church family, Beth hails from Cincinnati. Let's tell her how many churches are here."

The whole church responded in unison, *"One church!"*

He leaned in and whispered, "If there's only one church, then you are among family. Welcome home."

What if we didn't judge or form opinions about each other, leaving that for the One who sees our actions, as well as our intentions? The challenge of amen isn't always the internal fight I have to maintain my spiritual composure despite my own brokenness and fatigue. The challenge of amen sometimes is the fight I have with you, fellow soldier. Isn't that ridiculous? Think of all the emotional energy we have spent in our lives fighting with spiritual siblings who are one degree different from us. Or lost sheep we should be chasing down instead of chasing away. I am trying to spend more time mastering the sin crouching at my door and less time paying attention to yours. There's enough struggle out there already. Why don't we all stick together in this redemption story?

I was in Atlanta's passport control room, a place where international airplanes dump into a common area. People file along queues, waiting to be processed and allowed back into the United States. Last year a new system was implemented, where you can walk up to an electronic kiosk and begin the process. I was traveling with my children, and as we snaked through the line, I heard the staff shouting directions to confused passengers unfamiliar with the new structure.

"Families stick together!" one lady shouted.

I smiled and said to the kids, "I want her job. What a cool proclamation to make over this crowd."

As we waited for our turn to advance, I must have heard her say it again fifty times. "Families stick together!"

I spoke at that church to share spiritual insight I've long since forgotten (and venture they have as well), but I'll never forget what they taught me: families stick together. My denominational preference never came up. Whether I raised my hands or sat on them, I shared with them more than common geography. We shared spiritual DNA. We were all in the family of God. This community way of living takes the sting out of the hard steps of living amen. What if family looked less like keeping track of each other and more like watching each other's backs?

## CHAPTER 7

# BURN THE SHIPS

## *The Opposite of Amen*

*Am I now trying to win the approval of
human beings, or of God? Or am I trying to
please people? If I were still trying to please
people, I would not be a servant of Christ.*

—GALATIANS 1:10

W hen Solomon wrote in Ecclesiastes 1:9, "There is nothing new under the sun," he couldn't have written a truer
statement.

There was a season when we realized we were failing the
orphan and vulnerable students we served in Mexico by not
offering them counseling services. We listened to them and
offered lay counseling, but it became increasingly clear that a
more professional approach was needed. We looked around our

big city and found what seemed like a needle in a haystack: a highly trained, evangelical psychologist who had management skills and the ambition to not only offer his own services but also to help us build a program.

After a few weeks of observing the staff, students, and general ministry life, he rolled out his plan, which included counseling for everyone, classes, assessments, group therapy, and the list continued. We knew we had some catching up to do, so we dived right in, enthusiastically participating and leading staff to do the same.

How does the adage go—if only we knew then what we know now?

The enemy opposes gospel work and has used the same tools to kill, steal, and destroy since the beginning of time. I don't know why it still takes my breath away to see it in action.

Reports came in from him that first year, and progress was definitely made. We were all busy getting healthy. Although it was generally agreed this man had a difficult personality, no one really suspected anything evil afoot. People were opening up to him, confiding their struggles and stories, and meanwhile, he was quietly amassing his artillery.

God has given us our own set of tools for battle. One of those is discernment, a general perception something is not right. Some have it in greater measure than others, and although I am not one of those people, eventually the inner alarms started to sound.

More than a year into our relationship with him, he called a meeting of our top leadership to announce his latest insights about the ministry and unveil a proposed new organizational chart (since he showed us what a mess we were), now putting himself at the top. He was blinded and deceived by his own ambition, and there were no more hidden agendas, just a blatant grab for power.

Gold, glory, and girls. The people of Israel were warned about it in Deuteronomy 17, and it's the same stuff we've been tripping over ever since:

> The king, moreover, must not acquire great numbers of horses for himself or make the people return to Egypt to get more of them, for the LORD has told you, "You are not to go back that way again." He must not take many wives, or his heart will be led astray. He must not accumulate large amounts of silver and gold. (vv. 16–17)

It's the lust for gold, not the gold itself, that creates an endless vacuum and never-satisfied want. It's the power of glory, the elevation of self, the adoring fans that accompany high positions that cause man to pursue it at all costs. It's the hunger for something never meant for us that has toppled marriages, churches, and countries.

It's literally the same trap, set by the same enemy in the same ways, just told in new stories every day.

By the time we finally saw this man for what he was, there was plenty of damage. He had lied to students about the adults who cared for them, creating distrust and division. He broke confidence from counseling sessions and shared secrets, hoping to manipulate emotionally weak teenagers and exploit what he knew for his own gain. The fallout was tremendous, and in the aftermath we felt raw, exposed. It was a bit like letting a fox into the henhouse, and all us chickens were left bleeding.

I am sure it didn't start out as an evil plot. How does this falling ever happen to well-meaning, started-off-on-the-right-path believers? We come into the presence of God and get filled up. We are off to a good start. Then we go and pour ourselves out on behalf of people and projects we feel led to serve. But we forget to go back to God to fill up the cup again. Instead, we walk around to the same people we were just with and ask them to give us something back. What they hand us is dirty water, or what the Scriptures call "cistern water." It certainly isn't living water, and the stagnancy of it won't satisfy, so we frantically pour it out on everyone, hoping it's enough (which it isn't). Then, empty again, we go with cup in hand, and now they give us secondhand cistern water, and it tastes terrible. But at this point, its flavor is familiar, and we drink it, spit it back out, and repeat.

Eventually, it isn't enough, and we are hungry and thirsty. Our sin nature is ripe for a taste of something sweet, which sin can be for a season. And the first sip of gold, the first hint of glory, or the first touch of a girl hits somewhere not satisfied in a while, and we start the fall. Not one of us is immune. We have all taken glory for ourselves that belonged to God. We have all wanted for ourselves the luxuries of this world at the expense of another. We have all thought about, looked on, or touched someone we had no business doing so. This isn't about *them*. It's about us.

There is only one remedy: drinking deeply from God's cup. That's it. I can't spill my gifts on others and then hold out the empty cup for them to fill. It simply doesn't work. Only Jesus can fill our cups.

This enemy we battle is terrible. His strategy is to drive good men and women to make awful decisions. When the dust settled from this scandal, I thought about all the nuggets of wisdom I had once learned from this man. I wish it were as easy as someone being all good or all bad. It just isn't. I can't write him off. The truth is, he is broken like me, and in his brokenness, he allowed himself to be vulnerable to sin and then ignored conviction when it set in. In the end, he tried to burn down our metaphorical house, but he was the one in pain.

This man, who hurt people I love, needs my empathy and my compassion. He doesn't need me to judge or punish him. He needs me to visit him when he's sick, invite him in for a meal . . . Even the One who has the position to judge and punish doesn't. I am not saying it is easy, but I am saying it's what's required. I am a work in progress, and some of the mess this man pointed out in me he rightly saw. We have a choice: to see our mess and be diligent to confess it or to see our mess and be diligent to defend it.

I choose confession. It's the surest way to tear down the temple my self-righteousness builds in my name.

## LIGHT ALWAYS WINS

My friend Tom works in Haiti, and I have enjoyed the moments when our paths cross there. One afternoon, he asked if I would sit in on an English lesson with four gang members who had been coming around his home. They were asking for things he couldn't provide (money, a job, protection), but he was wise enough to know they were circling around, wanting what they didn't know how to ask for (attention, love, peace). He told them he wanted to get to know them better and suggested some

English classes as a means to do so. They agreed, and their first class was on the afternoon I was visiting.

They came into the small classroom where I was already sitting, and immediately I moved onto the floor, essentially sitting at their feet. I have watched enough National Geographic to know when you want to seem nonthreatening, you lower your position.

We talked through some vocabulary words. They repeated phrases they had heard from TV and music, and through a translator we clumsily shared a few moments that created a fragile connection.

Finally, it was time for me to leave, and as I stood up, I sensed the Lord prompting me to kiss their foreheads good-bye. It was a ridiculous move and one I silently protested. I had been careful with even making eye contact, but nonetheless, I gently took their faces in my hands and walked down the line, kissing their foreheads, with an awkward linger.

The last one physically reacted, looking like I had shocked him. He told our translator he had never had a nonsexual touch from a woman before. I met his eyes and smiled.

I stepped out of the room into the hot, Haitian sunshine, not sure why I was there that day, whispering prayers about their future. I'll never forget their faces, and I still pray for their fates.

The next day, I returned home to Cincinnati, feeling very ill. I couldn't get out of bed and was experiencing weird symptoms. By early afternoon, Todd and I were searching "bulging eyes" and "scaly skin" on an online symptom checker, checking off a list of illnesses for which I had been vaccinated.

After an hour of research, Todd looked up. "Beth, do you know what has scaly skin and bulging eyes?" he said slowly. "A snake."

Shivering, I closed my eyes, immediately remembering my kiss on the forehead of those boys surrounded in darkness.

"This isn't medical. It's *spiritual*." He confirmed what was dawning on me.

Later I received prayer from some friends, and within the same afternoon, my symptoms were alleviated. Light always wins.

Diving into chaos will cost us something. When we rub up against darkness, it clings to us, wanting to scare us away. We don't always have the luxury of seeing it hang on us, as I clearly did this day, but when we advance the gospel, we can be assured there is an opposing force.

I've heard it said we can sum up the whole Bible in two words: *come* and *go*. The *come* part is easy—come into his presence, come into the kingdom, come into paradise, come into my arms . . . The *go* part is more challenging—go into all the world, go make disciples, go and be reconciled with your brother . . . While *come* brings the deep breath, it's *go* that brings all the scars. We have to lay our lives down on the foundational truth that God will be with us in the going. When we bear scars, when we get hurt or sick, misunderstood or rejected, we share in the suffering of Christ.

As I decide to *go* (have coffee with the friend who is hurting, initiate a conversation with the new neighbor I have no time for, give away what is more comfortable to keep), I get opposed by the one whose agenda is not reconciliation but conflict. Our enemy wants condemnation over redemption and destruction over restoration. I can get halfway into a calling, and chaos will rain down on me. That's when I want to quit. It's easier to protect yourself than take a risk.

# BURN THE SHIPS

There's a story from Mexican history that always makes me think about how critical my attitude is when I want to quit. It's about the Spanish conquistador Hernán Cortés, who landed on the shores of the Yucatán in Mexico with five hundred soldiers and one hundred sailors in 1519. These Spaniards had been convinced to join the mission with one single promise: unlimited riches. They were challenged to take the world's largest treasure from the hands of the powerful Aztec empire that had been in power for over six centuries.

After a long journey from Europe, they landed in Mexico, and Cortés reportedly offered them a final pep talk. He invited them to take what they came for, the treasure. As he finished his charge, he historically demanded that before they enter into battle, they burn their ships.

*Burn their ships?*

They must have looked at him inquisitively.

In response he said, "If we go home, we'll go home in *their* ships."

They determined they would either return heroes or die trying.

Now, with ships destroyed and escape routes eliminated, they were left with no option for failure. The outcome of their mission determined their survival, and as a result, they experienced victory and toppled a dynasty centuries strong.

I admire the tenacity of these soldiers. They were singularly focused and completely devoted. They sensed their efforts as being life or death. What would it look like for me to believe the mission of bringing good news counted over all else? So often, I get into the battle and look for a backup plan (*where is that other boat?*) in case my declarations and best efforts are rejected, or worse yet, fail. But I do want to grab that treasure or die trying. And that means eliminating the escape routes and determining in my heart there is no acceptable retreat.

What I love about the historical figure of Cortés is he began his mission with the end in mind. When I first started out as a missionary, long before we had children of our own, I hosted mission teams and saw what picky eaters some students were. *I don't eat strawberry jelly. I don't like wheat bread. I want creamy peanut butter* . . . As a result of those experiences, I always switched up my own kids' PB&J. I knew I never wanted them to complain about their sandwiches at someone else's house. So one week we ate wheat bread, the next week, white. Some days we had strawberry jelly, other days, grape. Sometimes the peanut butter was crunchy, other times it was creamy, and sometimes it was all-natural. There was a plan. I knew where I wanted to end up, and I was intentional in the process of getting there.

In life, we cannot extract a predictable ending when it involves unpredictable people. A + B almost never equals C, and if it does, it wasn't because of you. So maybe part of my job as a warrior who has burned her ships is to be open, because the mission isn't always what it appears. I might be fighting for one outcome, when in truth, God is working another angle. I'd better make sure that I am regularly checking in with him, or else I'll spend emotional energy, not to mention physical resources, on a plan I determined was best. Keeping the end in mind means I know this path will get complicated, but I have my eye on the end goal, not on the moment. The older I get, the more it seems most of God's work is a rather long play.

## TO LIVE AMEN IS TO STAY ON MISSION

I raced through the Denver International Airport, caught between a late flight from Phoenix and my return flight to Cincinnati. I hadn't been home in days. It was the Christmas season, and I couldn't wait to get back to my family. I was running so single-mindedly that I didn't even notice there were two men rushing in the same direction. We all landed at the gate simultaneously, begging and threatening the airline personnel to open the door. "I can see the plane still there. Please, it's Christmas," I pleaded. "I want to get home . . ."

Nothing worked. When they refused, we each went our separate ways, pulling out our phones, waiting in help desk lines, and making our own plans.

My solution became flying into a nearby Midwestern city, and although I would be arriving after midnight, I planned on booking a hotel before driving home early the next morning. Not totally happy but satisfied I found the best possible plan B, I flopped into my airplane seat and closed my eyes. I heard familiar voices coming from the seats in front of me, and I recognized the men who had run alongside me to the gate. They were making a plan to rent a car together when we landed and drive straight to Cincinnati, putting them there around 3:00 a.m. One of them noticed I was watching and must have remembered I was in their same predicament, so he asked if I wanted to join them.

I hesitated, then ignoring the alarm bells going off inside my head, I asked, "Do you know each other?" I decided I shouldn't get in the car with them if they were friends or possible future accomplices.

"No, we just met," one replied.

I *was* desperate to get home. "What are your mothers' birthdays, including the year?" I demanded, narrowing my eyes in what I hoped was an intimidating squint. I gambled a guy couldn't be all that bad if he knew his mother's birthday.

Slowly they complied. "April 15, 1942."

"August 10, 1950."

"Great." I was satisfied. "I'll go in on the car rental."

I texted Todd as few details as possible. *Going to ride with a couple guys to Cincinnati. Can you pick me up somewhere around 3:00 a.m.? Getting ready to take off and have to turn off the phone. Check in when we land.* I shut it down before he could protest.

When we landed, one guy handed me his business card, telling me to take a picture of it and send it to my husband (who promptly texted back, *He could have picked that up anywhere*). And off we went in the middle of the night, snow falling steadily on our two-hour-plus road trip. I took the backseat because it seemed less vulnerable. The driver was a nice enough businessman. The guy in the passenger seat was in a reality TV show, and he was on his way home to visit parents who weren't thrilled with his career choice, or so he shared for the first thirty minutes.

After an hour of awkward small talk, the actor said, "Man, this is wild." There was a dramatic pause as he brushed his highlighted hair off his face. "I feel like I'm in some kind of eighties road-trip movie."

The driver and I made eye contact through the rearview mirror. *Was he even alive in the eighties?*

He continued, "It's almost like . . . I don't know, this will probably sound weird . . . It's almost like we are *supposed* to be here."

*Oh, shoot.* This was a classic evangelistic opening for any Christian. *Yes, we are supposed to be here,* I wanted to say, but which words should I choose? I knew I should step in, except that I was still a little jumpy and now was long past tired. *Really, Lord, how well can this go?*

*Bring light to his darkness,* I reminded myself. *This is always the mission.* He had just spent almost an hour telling us everything that was wrong, and now I had an opportunity to share with him what was right. Where I found comfort, peace, joy. How in the midst of my relationships, there was an otherworldly confidence. That was my role—not to perfectly outline the tenets of the faith, not to convince him of how he'd gone astray—but to offer him in the chaos he had just shared, a bit of the peace I had found in God's family. I paused before speaking, and now as I reflect, I realize it was my most favorite moment of that trip. I submitted to God all he had made me to be as a woman—vulnerable, intuitive, sensitive, affectionate, fierce, communicative—and asked him to use whatever strengths he wanted for his purpose. *Amen. May I sound simultaneously tender and brave. Please, dear Jesus . . .*

"It *is* like we are supposed to be here," I dived in, hoping to burn a ship or two. "I think moments like this happen for a reason . . ." It turned out the driver was also a Christ follower, and for the next one hundred miles, we quietly shared how our lives had been affected by trusting in a God who orchestrated circumstances like these.

As the snow and conversation fell into a rhythm and Christmas lights twinkled in the darkness, something extraordinary happened. I let go of control. I was in a car with strangers, talking about eternal topics and feeling like I was grabbing hold of a treasure my fear might have easily caused me to miss. I reflected on how mad I was, how much emotional energy I wasted trying to convince the airline to let me on the earlier plane.

When will I learn? When the door closes, look for a brilliant new story unfolding.

Most of the time, plan B is simply better. Stay on mission, but hold the battle plan lightly. Burn the ships, and keep aware of the enemy. Confess regularly. Offer yourself. Breathe. Tell the truth.

So be it.

# CHAPTER 8

# MEPHIBOSHETH AND A GENEROUS KING

## *The Confidence of Amen*

*I saw God before me for all time.*
*Nothing can shake me; he's right by my side.*
*I'm glad from the inside out, ecstatic;*
*I've pitched my tent in the land of hope.*

—ACTS 2:25–26 THE MESSAGE

I was spending the day in a marginalized community in Mexico. I had with me twenty or so visitors, and I was trying to train their eyes on the unseen. I told them, "Don't look at the houses around you. Look instead at their relationships. Don't ask about food, about how much or how well they're fed. Ask about provision."

We were ministering together, sharing meals and encouragement with the indigenous women. It was one of the scenes that made me so happy to be a woman. It was women of both cultures at their best, giving away their strength and remaining strong, lending something no one held in her hands. Sometimes when I see women being catty or competitive or feigning weakness, I can resent my entire gender. This day, however, we were focused on the exchange, on balancing the equation by not giving without receiving. I told them we do a disservice when we give and don't take. That might seem counterintuitive, but when we give and don't receive, we subtly say, "You have nothing to offer me." (And I get away with holding you at arm's length). It was a beautiful day of tender and vulnerable leaning in, culminating in a worship service.

The service started in a way familiar to the Americans, music and words followed along on a screen, hands in the air, soft swaying. People were practicing and mouthing words they didn't understand, but they seemed to sense their weightiness. Then my Mexican friends, first just one, then a stronger chorus, began to sing something off script. They made up their own songs in their own volumes with their own melodies. They sang in response to one another and to the Lord. Looking around, I could tell it made some people uncomfortable. I was mesmerized, caught between my two worlds. I delighted in the abandon of the women from this impoverished community, basking in the wealth of his Spirit. I also felt the dilemma of my American friends. *Do I sing something? Do I dance? Is anyone looking at me? This feels weird.*

Opening my eyes just a bit, I saw an American friend jumping up and down in the front row, who I am pretty sure only moves like that in exercise class. My heart filled, and my legs carried me forward to join her. As we stomped up and down in that church, we laughed and sang in two languages about a God who provides.

The ground vibrated with the moving feet of our small but growing company of dancers. Right about the time I was thinking, *We sound like a herd of elephants*, I remembered something about the animals I learned during the two years I taught elementary school. Bull elephants release a subsonic sound when they find water. This sound is detectable within a thirty-mile radius. Humans can't hear it, but elephants can, and they come in response to the call.[1] Once gathered, the elephants naturally begin to tramp on the ground, aware that water is below the surface.

As they stomp together, a phenomenon called liquefaction occurs. It's a scientific concept explaining how the vibration loosens the soil, liquefies the sand, and creates a collapse of the ground that eventually forms a sinkhole full of water.

The elephants literally tap into the water table.

With every respect to my fellow worshippers, it felt like the first woman who raised her voice signaled to the rest of us she had found water. As we moved toward her and sensed the water she was promising, the noise got louder, and the ground eventually gave way until we, like elephants, tapped into the living water source and all drank freely.

This surrender breeds freedom, and freedom tastes so good.

I like to sing in unison as much as the next girl, and order seems more natural to me than spontaneity, but I couldn't deny how good it felt to play in the water that afternoon. I found it curious that my team came here to offer, and yet these women, who went back to homes without electricity or men to love them, led us to a place some had never been.

Women knelt and confessed before God what they preferred

to keep a secret. They released control and danced with abandon beside ladies with whom they shared almost no common ground. What happened on that day?

There were exchanges going on all around us. Sometimes between us and the Lord, sometimes between one woman and the next, and as a result, we exchanged burden for peace. We had an overall spiritual agreement: "Amen. It is as he says. Amen. He is to be trusted." We not only surrendered our stories to *so be it*, but we recognized and celebrated that surrender in each other. I was as high as I can imagine ever being, but my drug of choice was love. We didn't care what we looked like, sounded like, smelled like. We only cared what *he* looked like, sounded like, smelled like. When was the last time I had been in a room with a hundred women who paid no attention to themselves or each other? It was *so* good.

There was a tender connection forged between shared spoonfuls of rice. Testimony came forth not only on what God had done in our lives to date but also on what we believed he would still do. Many echoed their amens to these declarations, simultaneously affirming each other and praising the Lord. That kind of day leaves you with hope. It's not something we offer each other; it's something we call out from each other.

Hope keeps a medical diagnosis or wayward child from taking us under. It's the best weapon we carry on any given day. It says, "I don't care how it looks or what I feel. I know this story isn't over. I know Jesus sits on the throne. I am bent here underneath it, whispering this word *amen*. So be it."

There are a whole lot of reasons I would have loved to know King David in his time. When the battle raged, he said, *I trust you for victory*. When his child was sick, he demonstrated, *I trust you to care for him, on earth or in heaven.* On days the treasury was full, he echoed, *I thank you for provision.* Whatever the circumstance, he was spiritually confident, internally settled on God's way. This surrender King David lived resulted in a pretty spectacular life. He would've danced with us that day, stomping for water. He would have sung spontaneously, and I bet it would've sounded a lot like, "I saw God before me for all time. Nothing can shake me; he's right by my side. I'm glad from the inside out, ecstatic; *I've pitched my tent in the land of hope.*"

# DAVID LIVED AMEN

Spiritual confidence is the outcome of living amen. It's an agreement between us and the One who has authored our stories. The challenge for me is allowing God the freedom to do his will within my life, which often makes me feel out of control and ask questions like, *What? Why? How? What are you doing? Why isn't it working? How come you didn't ask me first?* My challenges to him are all about my comfort, and his answers are all about my holiness. Why should I prefer a safe God to a risky one? Then I am just making God in my own image, instead of believing I am made in his.

I recently stayed in a cabin at Forest Home in California. The camp was founded by Henrietta Mears, who is credited with being the single greatest spiritual influence in the lives of famous evangelical men like Cru cofounder Bill Bright, international evangelist Billy Graham, and Young Life founder Jim Rayburn. That's quite a legacy. Outside the cabin where I stayed was a rock telling the story of a night in June 1947, when

Miss Mears gathered a small group of men for prayer. Together they had an intense encounter with the Holy Spirit, and the kingdom hasn't been the same since.

From this evening arose the Fellowship of the Burning Heart, a group of thousands ignited by a common passion to evangelize the world. The rock says, "Those who knelt in prayer that night were never the same and committed to being expendable for Christ." Overwhelmed with who God demonstrated himself to be, they weren't focused on their own inadequacies. They saw him as more than enough and themselves as his extension. Confidence doesn't come from getting better or sinning less, which can develop into pride. Confidence comes from seeing God as more than enough.

What I most appreciate about the biblical character David is how he didn't allow his own shortcomings to tone down the God stamp he bore. Much has been written about David—how he was unafraid as a boy, spent time as a shepherd, had the anointing of Samuel, desired to build a temple, brokered peace, slept with Bathsheba, had incredible military exploits. The stories fall on top of each other until they build a caricature of a man who doesn't seem remotely relatable. The Bible says the Lord chose David as king because he was "a man after his own heart" (1 Sam. 13:14). What makes that true, and how can we have that said of us?

As you read the story of David, you will frequently see phrases such as "David inquired of the Lord."

When David was told, "Look, the Philistines are fighting against Keilah and are looting the threshing floors," he inquired of the Lord, saying, "Shall I go and attack these Philistines?"

The LORD answered him, "Go, attack the Philistines and save Keilah."

But David's men said to him, "Here in Judah we are afraid. How much more, then, if we go to Keilah against the Philistine forces!"

Once again David inquired of the LORD, and the LORD answered him, "Go down to Keilah, for I am going to give the Philistines into your hand." (1 Sam. 23:1–4)

David was committed to hearing from God and knowing his will. He listened to messages through other people, whether prophets or priests. He also prayed and sought God personally. David's whole life was about listening to God and then obeying. That overshadowed his wayward thoughts and occasional selfish pursuits. God understands our weaknesses, but he won't tolerate our disconnection. He knows the more we listen, the quicker we understand what he's asking of us. When we obey, we demonstrate trust in his ways, and God can use our obedience to change more than we see in the day we're living.

One November Sunday I was visiting a Michigan church, advocating for Back2Back alongside staff members Rodo and Becca Arguello. As someone engaged Becca in conversation, I slipped her baby, Malaki, out of her arms and walked a few feet away so she could talk uninterrupted. I didn't have any baby toys with me, so kneeling on the ground, I pulled out my phone and we took pictures and played with the lights and music. I glanced down at a picture Malaki had taken of himself and noticed his dimple. It looked just like his dad's, and I was captivated by it. I closed my eyes and was temporarily lost in two decades of memories.

Rodo was the first Hope program graduate, which means he grew up in a Mexican children's home and then went on to graduate college. Along with many other staff members, Todd and I were personally vested in his life. We drove him to high school, and to be honest, it was not the most exciting part of our day. But sitting there I realized that while we were waking up and heading to the *Interamericana* High School, longing to see Rodo be successful, God had *both* Rodo and Malaki in his mind's eye. I could only see it (the task, the relationship, the assignment) from my earthly perspective, but God could see all the generations that would follow Rodo. He knew that young man would grow up to be the father of a little boy whose home would have parents who loved him, each other, and Jesus.

When I pray starting with *amen* and lift my thoughts and plans to the Lord, there's a confidence that swells in me. "God's got this" becomes bedrock, and on it sit truths like "each day holds great value" and "people are always worth it." This makes each day significant. There's purpose to even the smallest of details. God won't waste one bit of my offering to him. If I offer him my errands, he'll use them somehow. If I offer him my phone calls, my work, my play, then it all gets used for his glory. I realized how showing up every day set Rodo an example that presence matters. There is a spiritual assurance in recognizing that more is always going on. I pray Malaki will one day understand he's in a redemptive story written by a heavenly Father with big plans for us all.

Spiritual confidence, bred from surrender and not puffed-up pride garnered from mere learning, is marked by certain graciousness. It looks like, "I have plenty, so plenty I can share." There is an abundance mentality, and when expressed, it looks invitational. This kind of confidence comes from spending an extended time in confession, acknowledging our brokenness and radically filling up on his grace. It knows God will come through because it has seen him do so over and again. King David had experienced God's kindness and his undeserved favor, and he often acknowledged both by the way he treated others. Consider this example when he was unnecessarily kind to a young man named Mephibosheth.

David asked, "Is there anyone still left of the house of Saul to whom I can show kindness for Jonathan's sake?"

Now there was a servant of Saul's household named Ziba. They summoned him to appear before David, and the king said to him, "Are you Ziba?"

"At your service," he replied.

The king asked, "Is there no one still alive of the house of Saul to whom I can show God's kindness?"

Ziba answered the king, "There is still a son of Jonathan; he is lame in both feet." . . .

When Mephibosheth son of Jonathan, the son of Saul, came to David, he bowed down to pay him honor. David said, "Mephibosheth!"

"At your service," he replied.

"Don't be afraid," David said to him, "for I will surely show you kindness for the sake of your father Jonathan. I will restore to you all the land that belonged to your grandfather Saul, and you will always eat at my table."

Mephibosheth bowed down and said, "What is your servant, that you should notice a dead dog like me?"

Then the king summoned Ziba, Saul's steward, and said to him, "I have given your master's grandson everything that belonged to Saul and his family. You and your sons and your servants are to farm the land for him and bring in the crops, so that your master's grandson may be provided for. And Mephibosheth, grandson of your master, will always eat at my table." . . .

So Mephibosheth ate at David's table like one of the king's sons. . . .

And Mephibosheth lived in Jerusalem, because he always ate at the king's table; and he was lame in both feet. (2 Sam. 9:1–3, 6–10a, 11b, 13)

The world whispers in our ear to stand up for ourselves, to take what we deserve, to stick it to the other guy, and, most important, to look out for ourselves first. These messages are so prevalent in our culture that they've seeped into our churches. It's applauded when we think for ourselves, believe in ourselves, and take care of ourselves; it's even deemed mature. Jesus has always had another way. He says to stand up for those who can't defend themselves. Give away until it feels like a sacrifice. When our enemies ask for our coats, give them our shirts as well. Consider the needs of others as more important than your own. When we decide to make Jesus' way our way, just the otherworldliness of it all stands as a testimony. It's literally attractive. It draws in.

In 2 Samuel, the dying David looked back on his life and said how blessed he was. He never could out-give God. There are examples of David's blessing those who cursed him when he walked by and being merciful to wayward family members and sworn enemies. This kindness dignified his faith and provided evidence he lived by a code greater than this world. The result was more than material blessings. It was a fullness of spirit, a sense God made things right.

When I read about David's life and all he built, what makes the strongest impression on me is his acknowledgment of God's sovereignty. He wouldn't take credit. In this maker culture, where we are all busy building our own kingdoms, making sure our business plans are unique and well positioned, our products are perfect, and our homes are worthy of envy, David demonstrated his eyes were not on himself but on the One who made it all possible. He began and ended his ministry by acknowledging the absolute sovereignty of God in the lives of his people (1 Sam. 17:46–47; 1 Chron. 29:10–14). These are some of his last words before Solomon was appointed king and David died.

David praised the LORD in the presence of the whole assembly, saying,

> "Praise be *to you*, LORD,
>> the God of our father Israel,
>> from everlasting to everlasting.
> *Yours*, LORD, is the greatness and the power
>> and the glory and the majesty and the splendor,
>> for everything in heaven and earth is *yours*.
> *Yours*, LORD, is the kingdom;
>> *you* are exalted as head over all.
> Wealth and honor come from *you*;
>> *you* are the ruler of all things.
> In *your* hands are strength and power
>> to exalt and give strength to all.
> Now, our God, we give *you* thanks,
>> and praise *your* glorious name.

"But who am I, and who are my people, that we should
be able to give as generously as this? Everything comes from
*you*, and we have given *you* only what comes from *your* hand."
(1 Chron. 29:10–14)

At this point in his life, David was beloved to the point of
reverence. He could have stood before an audience and taken
credit for the kingdom, the treasury, and the peace, and all would
have cheered for him. Instead, in every sentence of this would-
last-for-eternity speech, he made sure all knew credit belongs to
the Lord. This was the secret to how he slept despite his flaws
and danced regardless of who was watching. Everything belongs
to the Lord. Spiritual Holy Spirit confidence doesn't come from
our own talents or accomplishments. It comes from an assured-
ness God has it.

And by *it*, I mean everything.

Including me.

## AMEN HAS CONFIDENCE IN
## WHAT IT DOES NOT YET SEE

I participated in a beautiful outdoor worship service last night;
it was a wonderful break in an otherwise stressful week. At one
point in the evening, I leaned back and looked up at the sky:
everything clear and the stars out. My thoughts floated to my
family and the conversations we had throughout the day.

We were moving that month (hence the stressful week), and
there was an added pressure to our home. I know the kids could
feel it. I was a part of it, as my emotions were all over the place,

and the kids were absorbing that from me. The going through of belongings, the saying good-bye, and the "lasts" of practically everything . . .

I wondered how they were going to adjust to the coming changes. *How will I adjust to the coming changes? Are we ready? Who is the most ready? Who said what today? What does that mean?* On and on the thoughts spun inside my head, as I joined in on the chorus of a familiar worship song.

*I know, Lord, you are reminding me to focus more on you and less on me.* The war continued to wage, my faith versus my fears, an utterly familiar battle; you'd think at a worship service, faith would have the home field advantage.

Then an older mother in the crowd came over to sit beside me. As she prompted me with a soothing voice and a simple question of what was on my mind, I shared my concerns about the move and the coming changes. She listened patiently, nodding in the I've-been-there-you'll-be-fine way older women do. I went on and on in the I-finally-have-an-audience-that-doesn't-interrupt-me way younger mothers do.

She waited for me to pause and then said, "Look up at the moon. Do you see it?"

Yes, I did. It was about a quarter full.

"See how you can only make out part of it, but your mind tells you there is more there?"

I looked in the sky and whispered, "Yes."

"I think that's a picture for what the Lord wants to tell you tonight. You can only see a part of this story, and so you worry. But your mind's eye is telling you there is more there, more coming, and it's going to be good. Have faith and listen for him."

I went still, all my humanity forced to settle. The deep

breath I wanted for that night came, and I found it remarkable that Jesus was capable of finding a place to root amid all the wild conflict of my soul. The very act of moving rips and tears apart. He knows. As plainly as I can say it, nothing here is forever. Part of my grief was over change and the loss of access to those I love. We were not made for this.

"Do you believe in what he has next for you?" she asked, not even expecting an answer.

My eyes filled, and I just nodded.

"Do you believe what he writes for you is good? That his stories for your children are good?"

I nodded vigorously now.

"Then trust what you can only see in part, believing in the One who has the full story. Allow peace to permeate your home and your children and your next steps. The coming story is good. There is more, and I'll bet inside, you know that. Now, live like it."

I hugged her, grateful for the word picture I will be reminded of every night during this season. The coming story is good . . . That's been God's punch line since Genesis. *Hold on, hold tight, and hold fast*, he tells us over and over in Scripture. *I am coming.*

A seemingly unconnected memory floated to the surface. In extreme naïveté, I once went running alone in downtown Tiranë, Albania, and got horribly lost. No cell phone, no language skills, no idea where I was. Hours later, as though he were in a scene from an overdramatic telenovela, Todd, my then-boyfriend, came out of nowhere, looking like none of the thousands of people surrounding me, and I ran to him. My only words: *"You came for me."*

Now I felt like the same young girl, a bit overdramatic but

still with a real sense of loss and confusion. Jesus came for me, and although the relief was sweet, it was a shadow reflection of what it will feel like when he comes for me the last time. I wanted him to know faith won this round, so in response I joined my voice with the others and worshipped with abandon.

I'm pitching this tent in the land of hope.

# CHAPTER 9

# IT'S BETTER TO GIVE AWAY A LIFE THAN TO BUILD ONE

## *The Lifestyle of Amen*

*Then Moses would return to the camp, but his young aide Joshua son of Nun did not leave the tent.*

—Exodus 33:11

I was in Mexico City, needing a cab to take me to the embassy. The hotel called a secure taxi service, and within minutes I was riding with Ignacio, a man who had been driving a cab for decades. Pretty quickly, we engaged in a spiritual conversation. He told me what was wrong with the church and with Christians.

I listened, jumped in where appropriate, trying to insert truth with grace. As we neared my destination, I concluded with, "Maybe the Lord brought me to your backseat today because he wanted to stir your spiritual pot. He is undoubtedly pursuing you, Ignacio."

He reluctantly agreed things don't just happen, although he credited fate more than providence, and we parted ways. I thought about Ignacio later in the day when I traveled back to the hotel in another taxi and prayed God would bring more believers into his backseat.

The next day, I found myself in need of another taxi. In this city of twenty-one million people, I raised my hand on the street for a ride, and a taxi pulled over to pick me up. When I slid into the backseat, I laughed out loud.

"*¡Buenas tardes!*" I exclaimed.

It was Ignacio.

What were the odds? Thousands of *taxistas* drive the streets of Mexico City.

"Oh, boy!" he said when he recognized me. "Now I know for sure God's gunning for me! Round two."

God gets our attention in many ways. Some moments are overt, like in Ignacio's case, when the intersection of the spiritual and our daily routine is undeniable. Other days it's subtler, and I have to strain to hear his voice. However it happens and wherever we sense him, when we stop and listen, we enter into what the Israelites called the "tent of meeting." It's ridiculously special to have a standing invitation by the Creator to connect on how I feel, what he wants, where we're going . . .

In Exodus 33, Moses went into this tent of meeting, a place where he and the Lord regularly talked about next steps. I imagine it was like a download, God giving Moses what he needed (wisdom, mercy, love, direction, peace) and Moses giving God back what he deserved (attention, devotion, obedience).

Moses could go into a specified holy space and be assured he'd hear God's voice. Today, it's less about geography and more about posture. I can hear God when I'm running, showering, or driving. I miss out on him when I delight in my own thoughts or listen to the radio or fill my mind with other voices. I miss him when I feel self-confident instead of dependent. Missing him is a summons to fall, and falling results in pain. How much of my pain or pain I've caused others could've been prevented by just listening better? A lifestyle of living amen begins and ends with intentional time spent in the tent of meeting.

I can hear God in the voice of a friend, a chorus of a song, or in the stillness of my heart. They are all notes in this big symphony God is orchestrating. I have established great habits of spending regular time with the Lord in the morning or at night but later broken them. I am not the kind of girl whose days are predictable or whose patterns are routine. This makes the practice of drawing in for his voice all the more critical. Left to myself, I would zigzag all over story lines God had written a straight passageway through. He promises to give us what we need for what is ahead. "Tent of meeting time" is the most important way to right my thinking.

Now Moses used to take a tent and pitch it outside the camp some distance away, calling it the "tent of meeting." Anyone inquiring of the LORD would go to the tent of meeting outside the camp. And whenever Moses went out to the tent, all the people rose and stood at the entrances to their tents, watching Moses until he entered the tent. As Moses went into the tent, the pillar of cloud would come down and stay at the entrance, while the LORD spoke with Moses. Whenever the people saw the pillar of cloud standing at the entrance to the tent, they all stood and worshiped, each at the entrance to their tent. (Ex. 33:7–10)

This next verse is why this passage is often quoted. It's amazing to imagine God facing us: "The LORD would speak to Moses face to face, as one speaks to a friend" (v. 11).

But the second half of the verse is the part I like best: "Then Moses would return to the camp, but his young aide Joshua son of Nun did not leave the tent" (v. 11).

Can you imagine this? Joshua followed Moses into the tent because that was what young aides did; they followed. He listened to how Moses led and how he talked to others. He watched this face-to-face encounter with God, and when Moses left to go back to work, it was so captivating to be in there, so intoxicating to hear God speak, that Joshua didn't want to leave.

When we flip in our Bibles just a few books over, we read all about Joshua's future adventures. He went out like a spy with Caleb, he fought a battle in Jericho, and he had all kinds of victories. I don't think his story would be believable without these details. Now that I know he'd been in the tent of meeting, I believe anything is possible. It's where surrender happens. In the metaphorical tent of the meeting, I lay down my children and their futures. I lay down sins I usually prefer picking up. I trade my wants for God's. I turn up his voice, so when the road curves, I lean in, instead of crash.

This is where humans get courage for remarkable acts. When we read of martyrs and their boldness, I assume they've just been in the tent of meeting. When I think of adoptive parents, faith-filled politicians, inner-city teachers, or hospice workers, I know the only way they keep going is face-to-face time with Jesus like a friend.

## A CHAMPION OF THE FAITH

I was late, running down the jet bridge and hoping I didn't have anything identifying myself as a Christian as I pushed my way to the front of the taxi line. I was coming into Miami from Haiti, my hair still crusty with the dirt and sweat from my ride in the back of a *tap tap*. I hoped it would come off like gel. I changed in the back of the taxi (no tip needed for this ride!) and tried to gracefully pull my backpack and suitcase into an event where I was speaking that evening. It was called the Champions of the Faith, an award ceremony for those who had made a remarkable contribution to an area of Christian service.

The honorees were backstage, prepping their speeches to thank publishers and producers who helped with their books and music CDs. Honorees included Christian business owners and folks who started hospitals in international slums with nothing more than duct tape and Band-Aids. I was not being honored. I was just the speaker, asked to address the crowd on the virtues of offering what you have to a larger kingdom. I knew what I was going to say, having prepared on the plane. I spotted the event producer, who let me know I would go on in about five minutes, and before I could get nervous, I stepped onstage.

Then I saw her. Sitting in the front row was Vonette Bright. Mrs. Bright was being honored with a lifetime achievement award for cofounding the organization now known as Cru with her husband, the late Bill Bright. As the tape would later roll with their story, more than sixty years ago they started an organization for students, teaching them to reach out to those who didn't know Jesus on college campuses around the world. Today, the international organization has touched tens of millions of people. She rightly deserved to be honored.

I had never seen her in person, just in pictures, and my first impression was of her expectant face. She looked up at me as though I were about to tell everyone a wonderful story.

I forgot my memorized outline about some passage in Mark, and instead I knelt down right in front of her. "Mrs. Bright," I started, "in 1993, my now-husband and I went to Albania with Cru. While we were there, we visited an orphanage, and I held for the first time a vulnerable child. My whole world changed. It stirred something that years later would be the impetus for what's become our life work, a ministry aimed specifically at international orphans. I pledged my heart to the nations almost twenty years ago while on that trip, and although we have never met, your life has had a profound impact on mine."

In John 14:6, Jesus taught that he is "the way and the truth and the life." I believe and am glad it's true for me that I can find the way, know the truth, and have the life. But I believe God showed me the way, so I can show others the way. I can find the truth, so I can tell others the truth. He is the life, so I can have the life and ultimately share my life. I was standing before a woman who understood the value of decades of choosing to share the life.

Mrs. Bright looked up at me, eyes sparkling, as if she'd never heard a testimony like mine before, although I was sure she'd heard thousands. There were some flashy characters in the audience, and I could have been really wooed by them. But I was captivated by Mrs. Bright, who seemed physically fragile, with a bedtime she later confided we'd long overshot.

God had something for me that evening, and I am glad I didn't miss it. There are some shiny apples out there in the world and in the church, and I am naturally drawn to them. I can be impressed far too easily by what man can do. Looking at Mrs. Bright's life, it is clear she was available and willing to lay down her own agenda in order to follow a grander plan, and the results speak for themselves. She makes a strong argument that it's better to give away a life than to build one.

## AMEN IS A CONDUIT OF LOVE

My friend Craig and I walked into the large multipurpose room in Mexico. It was already crowded as we picked our way through the bodies to find a spot in the back. Most of the room was filled with orphans who were now in high school or college. We had been in their lives since they were young, and Craig was a frequent visitor to campus. He spotted an older boy he recognized from years ago and nudged me. "Is that Enrique?"

"Yes, it is. Can you believe how tall he's gotten?"

"I'm going to see if he remembers me." Craig headed over to Enrique.

I stopped myself from joining them. I knew I could translate and make communication smoother, but sometimes the sweet effort of broken phrases and wild gestures makes connection happen faster than conversation. I watched from afar.

Enrique's face lit up when he saw Craig, and he pulled out his flip phone, showing him something on the screen. I watched with a half smile. Then I noticed Craig's face had suddenly gone white.

I moved through the crowd to intervene. "What's wrong?" I asked Craig.

He just pointed to the phone.

I looked down at the screen to see an old picture of Craig and a much younger Enrique, arms linked, sharing a day at the water park. I looked up at Enrique. "How did you know he was going to be here? Where did you get this?"

He smiled, like he was letting us in on the best of secrets. "I took a picture of this picture I've had for a long time. I keep it as my screen saver and look at it every time I pull out my phone. This picture represents the first day I remember ever feeling loved, and it's my daily reminder God loves me and can use anyone out there to show it."

I struggled through the translation to Craig. His eyes filled, and he reached out to hug Enrique, using more nonverbal vocabulary than I could have ever translated.

Love is such a powerful tool we wield. Preemptive love is possibly the sharpest version of that tool we have to offer. *Preemptive* means "serving to forestall something, especially to prevent attack by disabling the enemy."[1] When I think about the enemy's design for Enrique, it's one full of anger and resentment for his station in life as an orphan. He is the low-hanging fruit, the easiest pickings for a devil who wants to bring him down. God's plan to forestall that attack was preemptive love, a plan so powerful that seven years later, it's still a shield Enrique uses throughout the day to remind himself of truth. What would happen if we preemptively loved neighbors and teachers and people of another color? Would we disarm their natural defenses, lay down our own offenses, and make a space for connection?

The lifestyle of living amen allows God to take a day spent in a water park with an orphan and make something of it. It's offering our meals or our listening ears and trusting those efforts are being woven into something larger we couldn't orchestrate on our own. We are accountable only to love, to have an answer ready for the hope we have, to be loving, serving, forgiving. In the end, *so be it* says, "It's up to you to do the wooing, Lord, and the breaking. I can't convict or convince anyone of anything. I can't want for someone what they don't want for themselves. I can only regularly listen and then obey. Listen, then reach out. Listen, then offer." There's a lot of listening that happens in this God relationship, and as best I can tell, it happens in the metaphorical tent of meeting.

We are part of a kingdom greater than our own making. When someone spends time with us, in the end they should know more about Jesus and his character than they do about ours. Even after seeing Mrs. Bright for only twenty minutes, I know from her testimony that God is faithful, he takes something small and grows it, and he has a heart for the lost world. When we spend time with God's children, we should know more about him. God asks that when we love or speak or act in life, we do so for *his* glory. Craig must have done a great job of this at the water park. Enrique's exchange with Craig was so meaningful that it was the gateway to understanding how God feels about him.

Craig and I talked later in the night about the power of that moment and the wisdom of Matthew 7:12: "Here is a simple, rule-of-thumb guide for behavior: Ask yourself what you want people to do for you, then grab the initiative and do it for *them*" (THE MESSAGE, emphasis in original).

I told him I was reflecting on how some days I love from a place of duty or love because I am being loved back. Do those days, I asked him, have the same impact as the days when I love because God first loved me?

## AMEN FIGHTS FOR EACH OTHER

We were walking in a Nigerian village, and I was fifteen feet behind Todd. I was happily holding the sweaty hands of two village children when I looked up and saw him ahead. I pulled out my phone and snapped a picture. I later posted it on social media with this caption: *Oh yes, this is how I like my man . . . with a Bible in his back pocket and an orphan in each hand.*

We have celebrated more than twenty years of marriage, and with that shared history comes wonderful vacations, terrible fights, seasons of health, and seasons of sickness. We have had months on end of what-wonderful-kids-we-are-raising conversations and difficult days in between when we want to manage rather than parent them, just to make it all easier.

We've had regular date nights, and we've formed and broken habits a dozen times over. On our best days, it's our common practice to stop wearing any hat other than "spouse" after 9:30 p.m. If the homework isn't done, the laundry isn't folded, or the e-mail isn't answered . . . oh, well, we are co-missioning a marriage, which is a priority over all else.

Our kids get playfully shooed away and fend for themselves

after this hour, and while not everyone will agree with our method, it's simply how we've learned to recharge. We download our days, share our frustrations, and celebrate together. We put the effort into respecting, rather than judging, our sometimes *vast* personality differences.

It's a constant challenge to battle an unseen enemy and to stand back-to-back with each other in our daily war for God's best. Living amen is a lifestyle of offering each other more than we demand. We battle alongside, instead of against, each other. Living amen, surrendering to God's will, is a gift we give to ourselves and to him, but it's also a gift we give to others.

When Todd and I first moved to Mexico we didn't speak any Spanish, but we wanted to lead neighborhood Bible studies because someone convinced us that was how missionary living was best done. We watched VHS tapes from That the World May Know Ministries in English during the day so we knew the lesson, then invited, with carefully crafted flyers, neighbors over for a meal and a study in the evening. They came, as curious about us as they were about what we were sharing.

We showed the same video lesson we had watched during the day, but this time in Spanish. Afterward, we practiced how to say various questions: "What do you think about . . ." or "Which part resonated with you?" or "Does anyone have prayer requests?" People answered our questions in long-winded responses we never understood, and we smiled sweetly at them, hoping there wasn't any blasphemy or heresy being spoken. Finally, Todd said, "Would someone close us in prayer?" and then we served a meal.

I was pregnant and always feeling very sick. Even the smell of the meal being prepared was a struggle during those evenings. One night, I made a chicken and rice dish for our guests and served bread with butter and grape jelly alongside it. I left the room for a minute to retrieve the salt, and Todd followed to see if I was feeling okay. When we returned to the dining room, one of the men had taken grape jelly and smeared it all over his chicken and rice.

Horrifically, everyone followed suit.

I looked questioningly at one of the guests, who in broken English initiated he had been to the United States several times and knew this was how the dish was eaten, so while we were out, he instructed everyone. Nausea swelling, I glanced over at Todd to offer my best no-way-in-the-world-am-I-putting-grape-jelly-on-my-chicken look when I saw him happily scoop up a spoonful of the jelly to plop on his dinner. He caught my eye and winked.

That night I was grateful he took one for team. There would be other days when I would step in and do the same for him. This is giving-your-life-away kind of living. At times it plays out in big ways, when one is exhausted and the other carries the load, or one messes up and the other mops it up. And at times it plays out in small ways, like at dinner tables when the next right thing to do only one of us can manage. Whether the relationship is with my spouse, my coworker, or my child, the process is the same. I learn over and again that dying to my own wants and giving up my life always saves it.

There is a kind of gladiator fighting, made famous in the days of the early church, where two men would be chained to each other and a wild animal was released in the arena to fight against them. The contest would ensue while a question hung in the air: Could the two men work together to defeat their common enemy? Or would their own wild natures prevent them from fighting in sync? It was entertainment for the crowd, who were worked up by the spirit of the world and the sport of killing. They cheered and delighted in the death they would eventually witness.

Our enemy has the same appetite for our destruction and delights in the exact same game. We get "chained" together with a spouse or a ministry partner and share a common goal while the stakes are just as high. He seeks out those pairs who can't control their own wild natures to come together and fight back-to-back. He watches while they struggle to identify a common enemy and waits while they take each other out in frustration.

We've had seasons when the chain binding Todd and me together was the only thing that saved us. Throughout his letters, Paul wrote warnings and challenges to stick together as a body, encouraging us that there isn't an enemy in the heavens or the earth who can defeat us when we are of the same mind in the Lord. I wish chemistry were enough to keep marriages together. We have enough of that to power a small village, but it doesn't stop our sin natures from rising against each other. At some point, what heated us up can burn us. It takes seeing the other (whether the other is a friend, a spouse, or a colaborer) as a gift and not a conquest.

I don't think we ushered anyone into the kingdom the night Todd ate the grape jelly. Its spiritual impact on others has long been forgotten, but I remember. I remember a man who saw sacrifice as a way to both encourage and amuse his wife, and he took it. And twenty years later, I haven't forgotten his small act of kindness or how he fought when I couldn't.

# CHAPTER 10

# IN THE NAME OF JESUS, BACK AWAY

## *The Boldness of Amen*

*You, dear children, are from God and have*
*overcome them, because the one who is in you*
*is greater than the one who is in the world.*

—1 JOHN 4:4

*S*how up. Please, God, just come and show up. Help me tonight
*to be more truthful than impressive. Just come, Jesus. I beg*
*you.* It was a familiar prayer, almost habit. I have been saying
something like it for years right before I minister somewhere.
It always amazes me that anyone thinks they have something
to offer in these moments; yet here I am, this time in Atlanta,
like I have been before, sitting backstage, going over my notes,

157

begging God to fill the room with his Spirit. *Is it so I don't look bad or so you look good?*

I finished and waited for the peace that usually fills me, but instead of peace, I heard him say, "Beth, *I have been in Atlanta* a long time now. I don't need to come and show up. How about tonight *you* come and show up?"

God is not a parlor trick I can pull out or a genie whose bottle I can rub and hope he's up for granting my three wishes. He is a sovereign God who brought people to hear him as the loudest voice in the room. Now I start my days and enter every room with the prayer, *I will show up today. I will give you my thoughts, my efforts, my time. You use them as you please. I have an audience of One.*

## AMEN HAS CHUTZPAH

I was with a team in one of the poorest marginalized communities we serve. We were walking through the streets and inviting people to a meal in the church's soup kitchen. We passed houses pieced together with whatever garbage someone could find in a nearby trash pile. It's a bit of a mess there but no more so than any community I have ever lived in—just out in the open for our gawking.

We were gathered in the outdoor kitchen when something across the field caught my eye. No one noticed it but me, and I excused myself to quietly investigate. As I got closer, I realized what I was seeing and broke out into a run. There was a man striking a woman with a small brick, and others were gathered around watching. I didn't think, which would have stopped me in my tracks. I just dived in front of the woman, adrenaline making decisions my mind might have reconsidered. I saw the attacker's eyes light with rage.

"In the name of Jesus, back away," I said softly and in a language he didn't even speak.

He shook his head and moved toward me.

"In the name of Jesus, you cannot hurt us." I spoke with more confidence than I felt, and I heard the woman whimper behind me.

"In the name of Jesus, walk away." I kept repeating these phrases while he spit and cursed and gestured wildly, causing the people who had gathered to give him a wide berth.

Someone from the soup kitchen noticed I was gone and ran to where I was now standing, poised to respond.

I didn't break eye contact with the man and repeated my mantra in a low voice I am not even sure he heard anymore. I whistled for a taxi on the busy street and put the woman in it, telling the driver to take her to the police station.

The man was irate she was leaving and yelled his threats.

I stood behind the shield my words had created. "In the name of Jesus, leave."

He backed away, clearly under the influence of something altering his judgment, stumbling into a house and out of sight.

I realized I had been holding my breath and fell down on my knees, shaking. After the moment passed and my heart rate stabilized, I felt almost high. "Did you see that?" I said to my friend who had run over to us, who was also shaking now. "Did you see what his name protected us from?" I let out a yell, sounding like a cowboy who had just held on to a bull for seven seconds.

I know in my heart it's not a formula, or else Christian law enforcement would never die on the job and Christ followers wouldn't be taken captive in war or die as martyrs in persecuted nations. "In the name of Jesus" isn't an incantation we can pull out to protect us when we purposely walk into danger. I know that theology doesn't make sense, but I also know there was nothing about me to intimidate this man or anything that should have kept me from the receiving end of the brick he was holding. What I know is light is stronger than darkness. Spiritual strength is more powerful than evil wrath, and when we engage in battle, the only tool in the toolbox worth using is Jesus' name.

In any moment when we feel fear or find ourselves directly facing darkness, it's best to invert our prayers.

Amen (*My life is in your hands*). Dear Jesus (*Come and claim this space*).

So be it (*Do what you want here*). Dear Jesus (*I need you now*).

The resulting posture of the soul is trust—not a wimpy kind of trust, like "I hope it all works out," but a fierce kind of trust, a warrior's confidence.

A few years ago, I started a small organization with a couple of friends that offers fellowships to young women wanting to grow in their biblical understanding of social justice. Heroine Fellowship was born with the heart to give women a place to practice their voices in issues facing the world. I say to those I mentor over and over again, "People are always telling women to stand up or stand tall or stand out. But I say we should just stand back (which is very different than standing down) and make room for God to go first. When he does, the story always gets better."

In the end, I think God honored my chutzpah, a Hebrew

word that is commonly understood as audacity, gall, or utter nerve. I don't show it often enough. I wish I did more. My mind usually stops my mouth or feet before I throw myself in front of the proverbial train or down at his feet.

Chutzpah has been made a joke by *Seinfeld* episodes and pop culture, but it's an ancient word representing unwavering faith, the kind rewarded by God. Think of the widow who wouldn't stop knocking on the door of the judge (Luke 18), eventually compensated for her persistence, her chutzpah. Or in Mark, the story of a woman with chutzpah who asks Jesus to heal her child, not taking no for an answer:

> The woman was a Greek, born in Syrian Phoenicia. She begged Jesus to drive the demon out of her daughter.
>
> "First let the children eat all they want," he told her, "for it is not right to take the children's bread and toss it to the dogs."
>
> "Lord," she replied, "even the dogs under the table eat the children's crumbs."
>
> Then he told her, "*For such a reply*, you may go; the demon has left your daughter." (Mark 7:26–29)

Jesus values this kind of gutsy boldness. That's a good thing, since in this culture we have plenty of arenas to showcase it. He had chutzpah in spades, and because he is my source, the supply is endless. I don't have to worry about using it up. I can speak up and stand for others, believing peace comes quietly in some cases and boldly in others.

The key is holding on to what I know to be true. Or better yet, the key is first knowing what is true, then holding like crazy to it. On any given moment, there can be a whole host of voices battling to seem like reality, threatening me to shrink back, but regardless of what I see with my eyes, there is only one truth. And gripping that truth emboldens my faith. I choose to be generous instead of petty and thoughtful instead of selfish. I choose light over hiding and kissing to make up over holding a grudge. Each time those choices hurt, and most times they do, I tell myself they are just growing pains.

## AMEN SETTLES ME

A group of us hiked into the Huasteca Canyon, down to the base of a climb affectionately known as *via ferrata* (Italian for "iron road"). I was loving it, despite the fact we woke up at 4:00 a.m. As the sun rose, we put on climbing belts and listened while our guide, Juan, talked us through the day.

"You'll be following the steel cable, which forms the iron road, fixed into the rock every couple of meters, by hooking and unhooking your carabiners. In the beginning, you'll find the routine of hooking and unhooking laborious, but as we ascend the mountain, you'll appreciate the need to stay connected to the cable. Each time you release, you'll be vulnerable to falling, and from those heights, that means automatic death. Always keep one carabiner latched on as you use the other to reach higher."

We started up the climb, culminating thousands of feet in the air. I found a rhythm of holding on to the iron road and pulling myself to the next height. Juan was right; the higher we climbed, the more I felt needy for the safety of a handhold.

In the quieter moments of our trek, I reflected on God's truth, specifically on its strength and how it anchors me. 2 Corinthians 1:20 says, "For all the promises of God find their Yes in him. That is why it is through him that we utter our Amen to God for his glory" (ESV). God's Word settles me. It's why I can say *amen*. It creates a rest internally that feeds a boldness externally.

As I climb the mountain of life, through the relationships and experiences I enjoy and endure, it's God's Word, specifically his promises, that seems a lot like these handholds. When I hook onto a promise (I say it, pray it, memorize it, beg God to fulfill it), it figuratively pulls me up a few more feet and holds me there.

About once an hour, I tortured Brian, one of my fellow climbers, with my foolish antics. I let go of the handhold and joked about falling. As he gave me the frantic reaction I was looking for, I giggled, but inside my stomach turned to liquid fear, the way it does when I nearly miss hitting another car.

In life, when I let go of one of God's promises—by either forgetting its power or ignoring its truth—and the reality of a potential fall takes hold, fear ensues, and usually anger chases it. I become anxious or irritated, which isn't how he made me. I cannot imagine what life would feel like without the regular assurance of these handholds. You must get used to the feeling of liquid fear all the time and assume your anxiety or irritation is just "how you are."

God's Word is littered with promises we can hold on to. He knew the dizzying heights to which we would climb, and he offers us hundreds of handholds.

When I read Ezekiel 36:26—"*I will* give you a new heart and put a new spirit in you; *I will* remove from you your heart of stone and give you a heart of flesh"—I know this promise can empower me to say, "Amen. The work is his to do." When I read

Psalm 103:12—"As far as the east is from the west, so far has he removed our transgressions from us"—I believe in his mercy, and with this promise I can say, "Amen. I am not defined by what I've done wrong." When fear threatens to overcome my spiritual confidence, I remember Philippians 4:19: "And my God shall supply all your need according to His riches in glory by Christ Jesus" (NKJV). And then this promise reassures me; he sees my need, knows my need, and will meet my need.

I have many battles still to wage and plenty of reasons to need spiritual nerve, so now I always look for these handholds when I read Scripture. I want the deep breath that comes from knowing God is holding me up.

When we reached our destination, I looked around at the view and thought, *This is breathtaking*. I looked down at our route and thought, *This is terrifying*. Most days that's life: simultaneously breathtaking and terrifying. I can be in the middle of the most mundane task and see one of my children offer himself to another, and it's breathtaking. I can be in the middle of a conversation and not know what to say and feel God's insight come on me, and it's breathtaking. I can also face unknowns about my health or our finances or the future and feel afraid. What keeps me climbing? Chutzpah keeps me climbing. We need chutzpah most days just to ask, what can I latch onto so I can climb still higher?

## AMEN GOES BEFORE US

It was the fall of my senior year in high school, and I applied at a local video store to earn some college money. It seemed like a dream job. We could watch movies while we worked and were allowed to take home as many as we wanted each night. I hadn't been on the job more than two days when a man walked in asking for a look at the book.

"I don't know what kind of book you mean, sir," I answered politely. "We do have some magazines for sale, but mainly we are a video store."

He looked around and seemed irritated I was making him repeat himself. "I would like to look at the *book*. You know, the one with the skin flicks."

The way he said it seemed shady, and I realized what he was asking.

"I am sorry," I responded, a bit flustered. "We don't carry those kind of movies." I wanted him to leave, but practicing my training, I instead inserted, "We have other new releases if you are interested . . ."

He lowered his voice and growled at me, "I know you have skin flicks. I was in here already this week. Now *show me the book*."

With that, Robin, my manager, walked to the front and quietly handed the man a folder with titles listed inside. Stunned, I watched as she pulled the titles he pointed to from somewhere in the back and handed them to me to check out.

As I took his money and gave him the thick VCR boxes, my heart sank. Not only was I renting out my first porn movie, I knew I would have to quit.

My parents would never let me work there.

Later that night, I recounted the incident to them. "I asked Robin how many titles we carried and how often we rented them out, and based on what she told me, rentals are steadily increasing in the area. Don't worry. I will tell her tomorrow I am a Christian and working there doesn't fit with our values." I couldn't imagine any other solution.

"So that's it?" my dad challenged me. "As Christians, when we see something we don't agree with, we just run away?"

I looked at him questioningly. "Set apart, holy?"

He fired right back, "Salt, light?"

We sat quietly until he finally broke the silence. "If you feel God telling you to leave, obey him. But in the absence of that, I would say you might be there for a reason. I don't want pornography provided in our neighborhood, but who am I? I am just a customer of the store, with an option to boycott. You are an employee with tremendous power to make a difference. Instead of thinking of what you can say, why don't you see what you can *do*?"

The next time I went to work, I rented out five porn movies. Two of them were to someone I knew. I didn't know if my theology had room for this theory, but it seemed like God was pushing my buttons.

I went on a twenty-minute break and popped into the grocery store nearby to buy a folder that I filled with wide-ruled paper. Down the margin, I listed the numbers 1–50 and wrote on the top in bold marker, "Not here." I then ceremoniously used the same pen and signed my name next to #1.

After break, I requested to work the cash register instead of restocking the returned movies. My first customer was a mom with her two children, renting a cartoon. I hurriedly whispered to her, "I also live in this neighborhood, and I can see from your account you do too. I didn't know if you were aware that besides the movies on display, we also rent pornography here."

She quickly shook her head and made a face. "I'm not interested," she told me, sounding offended.

"No, no, I know." This was not going how I rehearsed. "I know you don't want to rent any. That's why I'm starting a petition to have them removed. Would you be willing to sign?" I pushed my folder in front of her and hoped my coworker wouldn't wander over to see if I needed help.

"Oh, sure," she said, signing her name under #2.

I finished her transaction, feeling triumphant.

She looked pitifully at my petition, now with two signatures. "I hope you get what you want."

"I just did," I practically sang back to her.

By the end of the shift I had twelve signatures, three rejections, and two people who excitedly asked to see our collection. (I hadn't counted on the fact I would be simultaneously advertising this private service with my efforts.)

I came home and showed my parents the folder.

"That's what I'm talking about," Dad cheered me on.

I couldn't wait for my next shift. It was the weekend when traffic would be way up. The signatures spilled onto page two, and I had to confide in a coworker what I was doing.

"You're going to get fired," she warned me.

"I don't care. I want to do something. Every day, we either make a decision to build the kingdom of heaven or give it away. Each time someone walks out of here with one of those films, it feels like we are giving away good ground. I want it back. Let's at least make it as hard as possible." I had lost her at "kingdom of heaven," but my pep talk fired me up, and the campaign waged on.

A month later, I told my parents the time had come. The owner of our establishment was coming for a visit, and I made sure I was working that shift. I didn't want to blindside my manager, but I also didn't want her to get blamed for my actions, so by surprising them both at the same time, surely he would see her shock and not assign her any consequences.

He came in, his briefcase overflowing with papers, and seemed pleased as he glanced around. Our store had experienced a healthy profit since opening, and he had no reason to suspect this visit would be anything other than routine. I followed him into the back room, where he was going to look at paperwork, and after introducing myself, I asked if I could talk to him. "I am willing to clock out or use this as my break," I started nervously. "I don't want you to pay me for the following conversation."

He seemed amused and motioned for me to continue.

"I am not comfortable with the adult film collection."

He rolled his eyes, and his prior amusement quickly turned to annoyance.

I pressed on. "And neither is this community." With that, I dramatically pulled out my folder, now full of hundreds of signatures.

He flipped through it, mildly impressed.

I was hoping for *really* impressed, so I upped the ante. "We are prepared to boycott this store, and in a tight-knit community like this one, you won't last long. I'll personally camp out in front of the store and pass out Blockbuster coupons."

That was it. All the ammunition I had. I wasn't sure who was winning at the moment. But I knew one thing: I stood face-to-face with something bigger than the man in front of me, and it wasn't nearly as scary as I imagined it would be.

By the week's end he had pulled the adult films from the store, and I learned something that would come in handy later in life. The enemy is much like the Wizard from *The Wizard of Oz*. Remember him? The small guy who stood behind a big curtain? He is all smoke and shadows. He uses people to further his agenda of stealing, killing, and destroying, and while he might *seem* big in any given moment, he's just a fallen angel with a doomed destiny throwing a fit. He only wins when we cower or freeze.

I was hiking with my family and a bunch of students when my youngest son lost steam. Aidan didn't have the stamina for the final leg, so he and I turned around and headed home. We sang our way down the trail, backtracking the path we had worked so hard to climb.

Suddenly, a man jumped out and put his finger to his lips, signaling us to be quiet. He seemed desperate for us to stop making noise. He motioned to the creek bed, where I saw a mama bear foraging for food with her cub. He explained he was a park ranger and was tracking their movements. "We need to stay here," he told me. "Don't make noise or movement. She'll ramble on when she's ready. She's clearly already smelled you, but don't give her any reason to look over."

My preschool son was active, and the idea of him holding still seemed impossible. My heart was beating so loudly that I was sure the bear could sense it. It was one of the scariest fifteen minutes I've ever lived through. Finally, the mama bear and her cub headed upstream.

It's tempting to have the same posture when faced with our spiritual enemy. Freeze. Don't make any noise. Don't wave a red flag in front of him. Don't give him any reason to prefer you to whatever currently holds his attention. But at the end of my encounter with the bears, what did I learn and reinforce to my son?

Bears are in control.

Bears have power and are to be feared.

Bears can really hurt you.

I wouldn't want anyone to get that message from me when witnessing an encounter with a spiritual enemy. No matter how loud he roars or how tall he appears, it's just intimidation. He isn't to be feared. Peter wrote plainly how to manage a life that confronts an enemy: "Be alert and of sober mind. Your enemy the devil prowls around like a roaring lion looking for someone to devour. Resist him, standing firm in the faith" (1 Peter 5:8–9).

Peter teaches us the correct position, and it isn't to cower.

Living amen is an anthem that sings louder than any chorus of fear. It says, "I don't know what's next, but I will march on. I can't see around the corner, but I will run headlong anyway. I can't control, don't want to manipulate, and won't try to manage what's not mine to hold. I care about one thing only, my connection with Jesus. I will protect it, find comfort in it, and nurture it. Inside this connection, I drink deeply from the cup providing me with wisdom, peace, and comfort for the curves in the road, the bears on the path, and the challenges ahead."

Chutzpah may cause you to cross a border, a street, or a demonstration line. It may ask you to befriend someone wholly different from you. Chutzpah and boldness may ask you to heap extravagant amounts of love on someone uncaring. It's made me speak up to strangers and try new skills. It's made me ask relentlessly for something and let go of other things. This audacity, gall, or utter nerve is not something I can muster up; it's something that bubbles over. It is the outcome of time with Jesus and is as available to me in this age and in this culture as it is to a woman living nothing like me or from a time long ago.

Boldness. Our world needs it now more than ever. Amen.

# CHAPTER 11

# REBUILDING OF WALLS AND RUINS

## *The Result of Amen*

> *I will restore to you the years*
> *that the swarming locust has eaten,*
> *the hopper, the destroyer, and the cutter,*
> *my great army, which I sent among you.*
>
> *You shall eat in plenty and be satisfied,*
> *and praise the name of the LORD your God,*
> *who has dealt wondrously with you.*
> *And my people shall never again be put to shame.*
>
> —JOEL 2:25–26 (ESV)

I t was 2011, and in Monterrey, Mexico, where I was living, 1,782 people were assassinated in the much-reported drug war. The cartel conflict had grown so thick that by the fall of that year, people were no longer going out at night for tacos, a true sign of a Mexican crisis. It was on one of those fall nights, a pastor friend, Salatial, had a dream. In the dream, Salatial was in a patio full of police, who were all on their knees praying. He woke up startled and wondered, *Do I even know a police officer?*

In the morning Salatial told his wife about his dream, and, curious about its meaning, they began praying for the local police force.

Salatial ate at a popular lunchtime diner the next week and saw a table of police officers. Thinking it might be a good way to make an introduction, he directed the waitress to bring him their bill. They later charged his table, demanding to know for whom he worked and what made him think they could be bought, and he reflected that maybe that wasn't the most effective method to make an introduction.

A month later, one October Sunday, he noticed several new faces in the crowd of his congregation. He invited them to come forward for prayer, and eleven men and women lined up in front of the stage. Salatial started on one end and prayed over each new guest. When he reached a man in the middle, he stopped and spoke into his ear, "I know the Lord has saved your life now two times, and he has saved you for this season." He then continued down the line.

Later, Salatial learned the man was the new director of police for Guadalupe, the million-person suburb of Monterrey where his church stands. After praying over a month for the police, he was so excited to meet his first officer.

He invited him for coffee the following week and shared his dream, asking if the police chief knew of any believing officers who would want to come and pray with him.

The chief responded, "You know I am new here, right? Your

last chief was murdered about a month ago. I am just getting to know everyone, but I haven't found a single one I imagine would be open to your prayer."

Isaiah 30:21 says, "And your ears shall hear a word behind you, saying, 'This is the way, walk in it'" (ESV). When I hear the word, I know I have only one choice: obedience. Blessing always follows submission, and chaos trails our rebellion. Salatial valued obedience, and sensing God's voice, he persisted, asking regularly if he could visit the headquarters. Finally, the chief relented. He invited the pastor to share for ten minutes the next Saturday at the change of the shift during the 6:30 a.m. roll call, explaining this way he could see all the men and women at one time.

When Salatial arrived the first morning, he walked through a patio to get to their main room and recognized it instantly as the same one from his dream where he saw officers on their knees. Emboldened by this realization, he spoke for five minutes, sharing the basics of the gospel. No one blinked or moved or raised his hand, but Salatial left with a full heart.

For the next three months, he continued going every Saturday, speaking for a few minutes about integrity and reminding them that they represented God's justice on earth and not to hurt those whom they were to protect. They were well-crafted, powerfully delivered, and prayerfully considered messages, yet he still wasn't seeing any impact. *Lord, is this what you had in mind?*

He sensed the Lord speaking to him: *Add worship.*

*What?* He must have misheard.

*Add worship.*

*Really, Lord? Praise and worship? Not only do these people not know our songs, but they have probably never sung together before.* Ever since those first days when I moved out of the country and felt my fledgling steps weren't adding up to much, I've found comfort in Zechariah 4:10: "Do not despise these small beginnings, for the LORD rejoices to see the work begin" (NLT). I have to constantly fight my results-oriented nature and trust the outcome of living amen is his to measure. When he says step, I need to step and not glance around to see if it makes sense, makes progress, or makes me look good. He is looking for my obedience, and he sees that as the outcome of my faith. Salatial focused on his call, and so the following results can get credited to God.

Despite his reservations, the following half dozen Saturdays he brought a guitar-wielding worship leader, who basically sang a solo in front of the group for a couple of minutes.

Then in January 2012, during worship, one of the sergeants fell down, appearing to pass out. Everyone in the room, trained as first responders, rushed over, but Salatial stepped in front of them, quickly explaining he recognized the sergeant was "overcome in the Spirit."

Regardless of how your church worships or what doctrine you assign to this experience, the testimony remains. Although this has never happened to me, I don't doubt its reality. This guy was overwhelmed by the Spirit, a Spirit previously ignored.

It was all the encouragement the police chief needed. He asked Salatial if he would come every day, not just on Saturdays, and teach a class on leadership, using the biblical character of David as a reference. "I think they are listening and maybe even internally responding, but they lack the leadership skills to exercise their faith in front of others," the police chief said.

During the following month they met daily, and God gave the police force of Guadalupe great victory in the war against the cartels, so much so that the military, who had been called in for peacekeeping responsibilities, was reportedly frustrated. Why was this suburban police force making more arrests than anyone else?

After twenty-eight days, a ceremony concluded their leadership class, and the police chief announced to the station what everyone already knew: in February 2012, not one officer's life was lost in Guadalupe. Not everyone understood what it was this pastor was offering, and they didn't all believe in God, but they *all* wanted whatever good juju he was bringing, and they immediately invited him to continue coming every day.

This is when it gets good—when the community of God acts, as Paul wrote, like a colony of heaven. When a group of people come together for a common goal outside of themselves, even in the secular world, we see results. When that group is fighting to advance the gospel and there is room for the Spirit to move, the results are supernatural. As Salatial sat across from me in a coffee shop, detailing the early stages of this story, he lowered his voice for dramatic effect and said, "This is the week in the story when the anointing went *boom*."

He continued, "I couldn't keep the pace. I still had my church responsibilities and my family. I knew I needed to get help from other faith leaders in our community." Salatial gathered a group of pastors and shared what had been going on. He needed their help, and he didn't want them to use social media to announce what they were doing. He didn't want them to invite the men and women into their individual churches. "*This is the church*, and I just want you to go and speak the truth." They passed around a calendar, split up the dates, and made plans to love the police force in their community.

About a month later, it was Salatial's turn in the rotation. He arrived three minutes late, and, in his absence, a police officer had walked to the front, filling the "pulpit" and sharing his heart. As Salatial rushed through the door and heard the officer's testimony, he stopped, stunned.

This ministry was growing roots.

All through the summer and fall, major shifts were happening in Guadalupe. The crime rate dropped, the arrest rates rose, area pastors served police families, and people once again went out at night for tacos.

A new mayor was elected that fall, and he gathered some of the community leaders into his office. "One of my first responsibilities in office is to give the keys of the city to someone. I have an idea of who deserves it, but I have gathered you together to talk details." He looked around the room. "Should it be you, Chief? Or you, Pastor? Should it be a volunteer organizer? Who deserves the credit for this massive shift in our community? As my first act, I want to publically recognize them."

No one said anything for a moment. Then Salatial spoke up. "Sir, if you are looking for who deserves the credit for what's happening in our city, it's Jesus. If anyone deserves those keys, it's him."

Incredulous, he said, "You want me to give the keys to the city to *Jesus Christ*?"

"Yes, I do," maintained Salatial.

"If you want to claim credit, claim it for God" (2 Cor. 10:17 THE MESSAGE).

On December 8, 2012, the mayor stood in front of his new constituents and announced, "It's for this reason, that I, Cesar Garza Villarreal, mayor of Guadalupe, give over this city of Guadalupe, Nuevo León, to our Lord, Jesus Christ."

The crowd went wild, jumping to their feet and applauding.

In the front row sat dignitaries from other municipalities around the city. They watched with shock as the citizens of Guadalupe cheered for Jesus Christ and looked around at each other, commenting, "My ceremony is next week. I think *I* will give the keys to Jesus Christ."

By the year's end, numerous other large suburbs of Monterrey had given over their cities in public ceremonies to the authority of Jesus. At this point, there were more than 140 pastors involved, and services were being held in police stations all around the city and even in key prisons and public schools.

Still, the downtown city police force of Monterrey remained unengaged.

Salatial recounted what happened next. "In February [of 2013], I received a call from the police chief of Monterrey, asking if I was free for the 6:30 roll call the following Saturday. Of course, I went eagerly. I am not going to lie; seeing hundreds of officers stand at attention while I walked through the basics of the gospel was a bit intimidating."

"What did they do?" I asked.

"Nothing, really. They didn't blink, raise their hands, or smile. I am not even sure they all really listened while I shared."

I paused, not sure how to encourage him. "Now what?" I asked.

"I'm planning on waiting a few weeks, and then I'll bring a guitar."

In June 2013, the Monterrey mayor stood in front of a televised audience of millions on the steps of the capital and shared these words: "I, Margarita Alicia Arellanes Cervantes, deliver the city of Monterrey, Nuevo León, to our Lord, Jesus Christ. For his kingdom of peace and blessings to be established, I open the doors of this city to God as the maximum authority."

Isaiah 61:4 promises he will "rebuild the ancient ruins and restore the places long devastated." The war in Monterrey wasn't between cartels, although they fought frequently, and it wasn't between government parties, although they clashed over solutions. It was—and is—an ongoing spiritual battle. It was exciting to have a front row seat to the revival in Monterrey, but not everyone understood what they were seeing. We woke the next day after the mayor's proclamation to mocking headlines: "If the Water from Your Kitchen Faucet Tastes Like Wine, Thank the Mayor."

What we don't understand, we rationalize or mock. God's hand is hard to understand. When what's natural doesn't occur—in this case, a bad situation getting worse—it can confuse. We expect conflict to break relationship, and we expect sick people to die. But the result of God's intervention is renewal, restoration, redemption, reconciliation, repair, and rescue. The faster I choose to say amen and trust he's in control, the quicker I participate in the remaking of broken things.

This story makes my faith swell. It's much easier to get overwhelmed with darkness and just surrender to the idea it will always be among us. But then I get stuck with managing it or trying to avoid it. How often do I juggle a mess of my own making when he's offering to intervene? Instead, I can believe God's Word that he has overcome the world and get busy advancing my communities toward the light.

I know his promise in Isaiah is for the rebuilding of more than just my city. It's for my own heart, which needs restoration daily. An hour ago I hung up the phone with someone who is sure all is lost for someone she loves, but I refuse to believe it. Why would God care more about Monterrey than he does about her relationship? He doesn't. He is actively working to connect, restore, renew, and repair what we unravel with selfish choices. When I was living in the Monterrey revival, or even now recounting it, what stands out most to me is this pastor's obedience. He had to regularly focus his attention on the call God gave him, the promise his labor was part of something he couldn't always see. I want to trust more. *So be it. Jesus, move in ways I can't always see. Amen.* I want to stop demanding such a quick return on my investment so that when it doesn't come, I won't shake my fist at heaven.

*Amen. You love (him, her, it) more than I do. You are pursuing them. Amen. I can trust you. Lord, I will always anticipate your turning things around.*

*Dear Jesus.*

## LOVE MAKES A FAMILY

God uses people to rebuild and restore. Sometimes I tell him about a situation breaking my heart, then sit back with an attitude like, "Okay, now. Go on. Fix it." Meanwhile, I think he's listening to me, aware of all the nuances to the story I can't see, and saying, "Okay, now. Go on. Engage in it."

This may just be me, but I wonder if God could collectively send us all a tweet, it would say something like, "I made you for more. Offer yourselves relentlessly." And it may just be me, but if the world could send us a tweet, it would say, "You are in charge. Protect yourself relentlessly."

When we go about the business of living in the light, of identifying ourselves as someone who trusts and surrenders and fights, it means bruised knees and sore muscles. Engagement in rebuilding and restoring is hard work, and commitment is required over a long period of time. I wish I could say pursuing Christ is lily fields and lattes, but it's not. I will never forget the dream that Amy Carmichael, missionary and author, wrote about years ago, describing the church as people sitting in circles, making daisy chains, while the lost were falling over the cliffs surrounding them:

> Then I saw forms of people moving single file along the grass. They were making for the edge. There was a woman with a baby in her arms and another little child holding on to her dress. She was on the very verge. Then I saw that she was blind. She lifted her foot for the next step . . . it trod air. She was over, and the children over with her. Oh, the cry as they went over!
>
> Then I saw more streams of people flowing from all quarters. All were blind, stone blind; all made straight for the precipice edge. There were shrieks, as they suddenly knew themselves falling, and a tossing up of helpless arms, catching, clutching at empty air. But some went over quietly and fell without a sound.
>
> Then I wondered, with a wonder that was simply agony, why no one stopped them at the edge. I could not. I was glued to the ground, and I could only call; though I strained and tried, only a whisper would come.
>
> Then I saw that along the edge there were sentries set at intervals. But the intervals were too great; there were wide, unguarded gaps between. And over these gaps the people fell in their blindness, quite unwarned; and the green grass

seemed blood-red to me, and the gulf yawned like the mouth of hell.

Then I saw, like a little picture of peace, a group of people under some trees, with their backs turned toward the gulf. They were making daisy chains. Sometimes when a piercing shriek cut the quiet air and reached them it disturbed them, and they thought it a rather vulgar noise. And if one of their number started up and wanted to go and do something to help, then all the others would pull that one down. "Why should you get so excited about it? You must wait for a definite call to go! You haven't finished your daisy chain yet. It would be really selfish," they said, "to leave us to finish the work alone."[1]

On my best days, I tune in this call: look for the lost, sacrifice yourself, draw strength from Jesus, and love, love, love. Unfortunately, not all days are my best, and I've spent far too many making daisy chains. But when I do tune in, the results are strengthened cities and strengthened families. The result of living in this spiritual posture is progress and connection and, most importantly, perspective.

Tonight I sat with a relative who has less than three months to live. I felt squirmy beforehand. I knew the basic rules. Don't avoid "the conversation." It's why he wants to meet, and it's all he's thinking about. Don't obsess, though, with the conversation. There's no way he can want to say the same things over and over again.

Much has been written on the Celtic concept of "thin places," a stretching of time so fine that you struggle to distinguish the eternal from the temporal. We spent an evening in this thin place, and Tom had eyes that held a grace evidencing he was getting used to the air up there.

We talked about the first memories we had of each other. He is older than I am, so his memory of me was as a little girl, visiting my grandparents who were his next-door neighbors. I told him he was the first person I remember considering as family who really wasn't. I always assumed he was a cousin or an uncle, as his family gathered in our homes, attended weddings and funerals, and acted like we had a connection worth protecting. I must have been in high school when I realized he was just my grandparents' neighbor.

We've now spent a couple of decades inviting nonrelated persons into my community and calling them family. It's been a powerful experience to metaphorically wrap my arms around someone and say, "Welcome. You are worth it. I see you."

As we said good-bye, I told him I remembered my dad explaining to me the reason they were family was because of the love they shared with my grandparents. I got the message loud and clear. *Love makes a family.*

"I don't know how windows work in heaven," I said as we parted. "So when you see my dad, will you tell him I took that idea and ran with it?"

From the very first time I sat in a NASCAR chapel, I was in over my head. I had met the NASCAR chaplain with Motor Racing Outreach on a K-LOVE cruise and agreed to address the drivers and the racing community in a prerace chapel at the Kansas Speedway. I walked around learning new vocabulary, words about racing and engines I had never heard before. I learned coaches are crew chiefs and huddles are pit crews. As I shook hands and took in this new environment, I tried to imagine myself in a car, racing fast, living life so on display. Although I am known among my friends as a reckless driver, this was a whole new level. *What do I possibly have to share that makes any sense to people whose lives are so different from mine?*

The drivers filed in, most wearing fire suits and game faces. They race on Sundays and travel most weeks, and this was their church. As I looked at their faces, I realized I didn't need to impress them with my stories of orphans or exotic foreign locales. In our testimonies, we need to share less of what we think God has for someone else and more of what God has had for us.

Facing those drivers, I couldn't pretend not to see the pedestal that people put them on. We were surrounded by tens of thousands of fans who knew their names and would cheer on their efforts later that day. The world they lived in was impressive, and to act otherwise would lessen my credibility and my representation of him.

I took a deep breath and shared about a God who moved mountains and healed bodies. I testified about lost causes and broken dreams being his specialty. God had the attention in the room. Only he could calm or convict or encourage us all. Every time I open my mouth to my kids, with my friends, or on a stage, I have one role . . . to testify. He does all the impressing.

"I can say with confidence, God is good. God can be trusted. God is perfectly on time. God is with us and for us." I shared with a confidence not born from my view of *me*, but born in my understanding of *him*. I can walk in this grace, not needing to perform or posture, precisely because he is high and lifted up. As hard as man tries, no kingdom we build, however impressively it's constructed, will compare.

Later, I donned earplugs and watched the pit crews perform in sync to change tires and make adjustments. I, too, cheered as drivers I knew and some I didn't closed gaps, drafted into position, and raced across the finish line. I thought about how diverse and creative and interesting our God is that he knows the details of the racing industry and uses what's important to the people in this world to reveal himself. He's simultaneously doing it in the world of those who love science and animals and cooking. He reveals himself to those who fight for justice, teach in classrooms, and operate on bodies. He knows every detail of every realm we might walk into *anywhere*. He shows off and demonstrates his interest and works within the context and community to say the same thing over and over again: "I love you. I see you. I forgive you. I plan for you. I hope for you."

I don't have to know about racing. I just need to know how God feels about racers. Replace that with anyone whose path he crosses with yours. I don't have to know about immigration. I just need to know how God feels about immigrants. I don't need to know about homosexuality. I just need to know how God feels about homosexuals. I don't need to know about the stock market. I just need to know how God feels about traders.

I left that first race feeling grateful I didn't need to keep up and be conversant in what I didn't yet understand. *He* is all wisdom, and *he* is all revelation. He speaks through us to anyone, anywhere he wants to deliver his life-saving message.

Amen.

# CHAPTER 12

# DEAR JESUS

## *The Community of Amen*

*God sets the lonely in families.*

—Psalm 68:6

I was driving down I-71, enjoying the sunshine and the quietness of my car. We had just moved back to the States after more than a dozen years away, and I was heading to a furniture outlet.

The phone rang, and from the caller ID, I recognized it as an international call.

*"Buenas tardes, Beth. Soy Perla."*

During the call, I was asked to act as a liaison between Mexican child services and US adoption agencies, helping to find families for legally defined "difficult to place" children. I arranged travel to Mexico to help create dossiers and eventually found myself spending a day meeting wonderful children with medical conditions and traumatic backgrounds.

As the day was winding down, I looked at the last name on the list: a boy, eleven years old. *He will be the hardest to place.*

I wasn't prepared for who walked in: this stunning young man with plenty of hair gel and swagger. As we made eye contact, the Spirit leapt inside me. *Who is this?* I wondered.

"Beth has come to interview you," started Lily, his psychologist, "but I think it would be best if we started with you interviewing her."

I was listening to both the boy and the Holy Spirit, curious about the reaction I was having to him. I cocked my head, wondering what kind of divine appointment I had just walked into.

He gazed at me just as curiously and fired off questions about whether boys play soccer in the United States, when it snows, and if pets really have their own beds.

"I think these are good questions, but I bet you have more on your mind," Lily prompted after a bit.

We sat a good while in silence. "I guess I was really wondering . . ." He hesitated, blinking hard. "I have never seen a happy adoptive family. My questions is, have you?"

"Oh, buddy." My voice lowered, and my defenses followed. I reached for my phone. We had just attended a wedding the weekend before, and I had captured many photos of our family together. "Look here at *my* adoptive family. I have kids from Mexico, and my brother has some from Ethiopia . . ."

He took my phone and scrolled through the pictures. There were images of cousins in three colors, playing games and dancing, making faces and hanging all over each other.

"Last names don't make a family. Bloodlines don't make a family." I forced eye contact. "*Love* is what makes a family."

His answer was swift. "Then find me a family like that."

*I think I just did.*

By the time I had flown home the next day, I had talked myself out of it. *Ridiculous. I can hardly handle what I am already managing. I will find him a great family.* I spent the next two months actively trying to talk others into adopting him. I found it hard to pray about him. Looking back, I can't believe how much I silenced God's voice on this subject. I stubbornly stayed in disobedience, making it look pretty with words like *margin* and *balance.*

Then one morning when Todd was running, the Lord nudged him. He came in the door and said, "Beth, I can't stop thinking about that boy. He's sitting in an orphanage while we are here, with all of this." He motioned around the house.

I burst into tears. They had been dammed up for a while. As I had been talking to potential families I would suppress them, but in that moment, I didn't hold back. "I know! I know, I know, I know. I am afraid. But I *know. Yes.*"

A lot can happen when we say yes. Later we pulled our kids into the room, walked them through this story, and asked if they, too, heard the calling.

"It's different with an older child," I said to them. "If we started out while he was young, I would have time to teach, model, encourage, train, but at this point, I am going to need a full-court press from all of you. You'll need to set good examples and love on him and join in on this journey as colaborers. I don't even know if that's fair, but I do think it's critical."

Months and months passed as we gathered our blood types and bank balance, friends' reference letters, and every other piece of documentation you can imagine to comply with arduous adoption requirements. Then finally, six months later, it was time to let this boy, later named Tyler, know we had found him a family. I flew to Mexico and arranged with the government facility where he was living for him to stay home from school.

He saw me immediately as he turned the corner.

"Do you remember who I am?" I started, feeling the emotion rising in my throat.

He nodded slowly.

"Do you remember what I said I was going to do?"

"Find me a family," he answered, not breaking eye contact, challenging.

"Well, I did. I found you a family. It's me! *Me!* I am going to be your mama."

I don't know what I imagined would happen. Maybe a hug or a shout. Instead, he doubled over, going into shock. Head between his knees, he began to have trouble breathing.

The psychologist was called in, and she asked him to identify how he felt. "Don't try and say much. Just with one word, how are you feeling?"

Tyler looked right at me. "*Alegría.*"

"Total joy? Me too! That's great. We can work with *alegría.*"

Saying amen means entering in and raising my hand. It's reminding myself on the days when his chaos rubs up against my barely held together peace that God started this story on top of *alegría.* If I let him, it's a gift he'll keep giving. There is a reason this boy and I are family, and I need my community to remind me of that. If the next years are great with him, I will be thrilled God thought enough of me to write great into my story. If the next years with Tyler are terrible, it's still all okay. God will stretch my muscles, he will grow my faith, he will convict me of sin, and he will teach me about trust and faith. So be it. I say yes.

As we've walked through the so-be-it lifestyle, our study of amen has revealed its varied usage throughout Scripture. In the Old Testament, we've seen it as the acceptance of a curse. It's also been the congregational response of affirmation or agreement in both Hebrew and Greek gatherings, the expression of praise to the Lord (think of the Psalms) or the characteristic of who he is (as "The God of Amen"). Finally, we've seen it throughout the early church as the confirmation of a blessing (as in Galatians 6:18: "The grace of our Lord Jesus Christ be with your spirit, brothers and sisters. Amen").

When someone embraces this word and uses it with the solemnity it deserves, there is a sense of settle that follows. I accept. I affirm. I praise. I bless. It testifies in two syllables to the conviction that God's way is best. We might not always understand his ways, and certainly we might not always like them, but we can always be confident of them.

During the year we were waiting on Tyler's adoption to be finalized, we would Skype with him every few days. Toward the end, it was getting harder for him to have hope the finish line would eventually appear. News of setbacks and delays would regularly discourage. I taught him that when I don't like what's happening around me, I remind myself of what is true. In our story, there were three things I knew for sure to be true:

he was our son,
we were coming for him,
and God had a plan.

We might not always understand it or even like it, but we can trust it. We would hang up our calls repeating this tune until his smile was the last thing I saw.

The time came for us to appear before the judge, and because Tyler was twelve years old, he had to speak before the court, explaining why he was certain this adoption was in his best interest. The stakes were high, and he was very nervous. He had been disappointed so many times before and had fear written all over his face.

"Why do you think this family is right for you?" the court official asked.

Tyler blinked repeatedly and struggled to find his voice. Silence hung in the air. He looked over at me, and I tried to smile in a reassuring way.

As Todd placed his hand on his back, Tyler found the courage to say slowly, "Because I am their *hijo*. And they came for me. God has a plan, and we will trust it." When it mattered most, he had an answer.

Truth brings peace, and peace brings confidence. *This is good.* I need community around to remind me of these truths in critical moments when lies are simpler to grasp. On any given day, I might listen to the lie singing its song in my head: "I can't do this." Or "It's never going to get better." Or "I am not enough." This is when your people can gather around and say, "Nothing is too difficult for God." Or "In him, all things are possible." Or "We are more than conquerors . . ." These simple truths pierce through the lies like double-edged swords and recalibrate my thinking and thus my living.

Whenever God expands my borders, there is a stretching period when capacity adjusts and boundaries reestablish. When I tackle it in the flesh, it can mean overworking and fatigue

(*Does God think I can really handle this?*), but when I submit to his plans and to the rhythm that comes from abiding in him, it feels more like surrender (*Where you go, I go*): "Whether we like it or not, *we'll do it*. We'll obey whatever our GOD tells us. Yes, count on us. *We'll do it*" (Jeremiah 42:6 THE MESSAGE). This verse conjures up images of hands in the air—"Pick me!"—and a sense that whatever God calls me to, whomever he calls me to love, "I'll do it!" I'll learn new methods, meet new neighbors, read more books, whatever, whenever, however he asks. *I'll do it.*

These days, I am working on wanting my hand in the air. I want to be called up to duty, I want a better story for my day than I can write myself, and I want the feeling I am at the end of myself and need him for my words, my next step. On our way to wherever he calls and whatever he asks, we will need each other. I need to be reminded that I want my hand in the air to "yes" when it doesn't make sense and isn't comfortable. I want "yes" if it means I stretch and grow and break and rebuild. It will be messy, but maturation usually is.

As a result of adopting the live-amen lifestyle, my blood pressure rarely rises when planes are late or grades aren't perfect. Life is sure complicated, and I am admittedly comfortable with complicated, but God still sits on the throne and can forgive me when I'm wrong and fill me when I'm empty. I am learning to shrug when dinner burns or the movie wasn't worth the ticket price, because here are the facts: God is good. I am his child, and he is coming for me. He has a plan, and I can trust it. This has led to many happy detours, serendipitous conversations, and plan B days. It has led to relaxed children, less conflict, better sleep, deeper thoughts, less wrinkles, and profound trust.

It's not really the goal, but frankly, it has led to happiness.

## AMEN REMEMBERS

A sense of self, and all that goes with it, has been rearing itself since the garden of Eden. Self-absorption, self-assured, self-conscious, self-deceit, self-doubt, self-flattery, self-help, self-importance, self-indulgent, self-justification, self-made, self-pity, self-pleasure, self-reliant, self-righteous, self-sufficient, selfish . . . the list goes on. We've made businesses, built cultures, and written books ad nauseam about how to stand up for yourself, pull yourself up by your bootstraps, look within, and self-improve. It has fostered, even within the faith community, a respect for independence and individuality. We've been sold the lie freedom comes from self-government, a reliance on only one person: *you.*

God's way is distinctly different and always has been. He tells us the way to victory comes through death, the way to treat our enemy is by love, and the first shall be last. His way is community, reliance on each other, and submission to one another. He taught us to be at peace with one another and to wash each other's feet. Through Paul he said be devoted to one another and honor one another above ourselves. Live in harmony and stop passing judgment. Instruct one another, accept one another, wait for one another, serve one another, carry the other's burden, be patient, kind, compassionate, forgiving, encouraging, and hospitable. This is how they'll know we are his kids. He taught the whole will be stronger when the parts work together and how to see ourselves as parts of one body.

When people come together to live this way, it forms an attractive community. It invites, it engages, and it is inclusive. This kind of community rewards people when they take big risks. It cheers on perseverance through a hard marriage, a difficult child, or any long-term assignment. In community, people fight for each other and pour out into their relationships what God is filling up in them. This is always how God intended for us to live, and yet to do so, it requires a basic acceptance that God's ways are best. The amen way of life boils down to acceptance. *I accept, God, what you say. I accept where this is going and what you have next for me.* When I accept God's plan for me publically, it's called a testimony. A community who eyewitnesses my testimony affirms these beliefs and encourages my faith.

This gospel, which was first expressed toward me and is now expressed through me, was meant to be lived, not just believed. John 13:34–35 says, "A new commandment I give to you, that you love one another: just as I have loved you, you also are to love one another. By this all people will know that you are my disciples, if you have love for one another" (ESV).

My friend Dr. David Schooler is fond of saying, "Restoration and healing are found in the margin." I can't fix what's broken in the world, but I can let God heal *me*. I can create margin so he has space in my life to work. When I see epidemics like the orphan spirit spread, I humanly try and concoct solutions. But this isn't to be solved; it's to be repaired. There's only one repairer of broken walls, and he does his best work when we rest in him.

I recently saw a meme on social media with the words, *No one else is your problem*, and below were loads of affirming comments. I was immediately annoyed by it, but it took a while to put my finger on why. Then I realized it too easily lets us off the hook. I may not be responsible for other people's problems, but I am responsible to those people. I am responsible to love well, speak truth, offer mercy, encourage, lift up, pray for, sacrifice, and honor, and the list goes on. As a Christ follower, I don't get the luxury to close my eyes to the problems of a billion children or the problems of my sister. If they hurt, I hurt. That's part of the privilege of carrying a God stamp.

Love isn't something God feels or does, and so by consequence, love isn't something I should just feel or do. Love is something he *is*, and love is something I can be. When I orient myself to this truth, my spiritual muscles relax in surrender. I am to be loving and exactly who he created in his image, nothing more or less. This eliminates the shoulds and the shames. It enters into the equation the spirit of "Yes, Lord." As I love others, it's as a vessel of the One whose love knows no bounds. He teaches the lessons, he guides the growth, he finds the lost, he strengthens the weak, he holds us up, he turns us around, and he grows the fruit.

See the pattern? It's all on him.

Our charge is not only to say, "Yes, Lord," but to find others who remind us frequently of the wisdom behind our yes.

If God's way is the best way to live, why do I rebel? I am prone to learning things the hard way and questioning just about everything. I have thoughts I shouldn't, and I say things better left unsaid. Still, he comes for me. Still, he writes me into his story. Since the very beginning, God's pursuit of us in our rebellion is evidence enough for me that he is from another world. He has forgiven his people and started again with a remnant so many times that I can't help but believe his mercy has no limit.

I love studying the Minor Prophets. They all start out about the same, with God's people making good choices, then making bad choices, then no longer listening to his warning. Finally, he sends someone from outside the community to get their attention, and the prophet speaks truth they initially reject and vehemently deny. Eventually, a group of God's people come together and acknowledge their conviction to each other. From this assembly, he rebuilds and begins again. He's doing it now. He's calling out to his church to stand up and not blend in. He's asking us to live like we are citizens of another place. I want to live among this remnant. I want to practice surrounding myself with people who acknowledge his voice and respond to his discipline.

His final words in the Old Testament come to us from the prophet Malachi. Malachi was speaking the truth to God's people about the way they were living, and finally there was a response:

> Then those who feared the LORD talked with each other, and the LORD listened and heard. A scroll of remembrance was written in his presence concerning those who feared the LORD and honored his name.
>
> "On the day when I act," says the LORD Almighty, "they will be my treasured possession. I will spare them, just as a father has compassion and spares his son who serves him. And you will again see the distinction between the righteous and the wicked, between those who serve God and those who do not." (Malachi 3:16–18)

It's time for us to write a scroll of remembrance, a record of where we feel convicted, what we believe to be true, and how we hear God calling us. It's time to acknowledge his ways are true, to ask forgiveness for the times we honor our own agendas over his. Amen. It needs to include lessons and mile markers along our spiritual journeys, moments when he stretched us and filled in the gaps our own weaknesses created. This record will benefit us on days when we forget where we've been and our appetites get the best of us. It's a gift we'll give ourselves and each other, and it can be left behind to encourage the saints yet to come. It should read like one long *so be it* and have the sound of surrender embedded in each line. In the end, all that we write, all that we've done, and all that we are comes from him. It's with him and by him that we cry out, "Dear Jesus . . ."

# THE QUARRY FROM
# WHICH WE'VE BEEN CUT

One evening my teenage son Evan complained of stomach pain. I thought he just didn't want to go to school the next day, and I told him he'd be fine. I sent him the next morning, and it wasn't an hour before the school called for me to pick him up. As soon as I saw him, I knew something was terribly wrong, and we rushed to the hospital for answers. After several tests, they confirmed it was his appendix, and we made plans for surgery later that morning.

While we were sitting there quietly, him sedated with drugs, me quiet with worry, he hit my arm hard, eyes wide. "It's getting worse," was the last thing he said before crying out in pain.

I called for the nurses, who confirmed his appendix had just ruptured and the surgery we were waiting for was now an emergency.

They rushed him down the hall on a gurney, and I ran alongside. The nurse asked questions about medical history, and I responded as fast as I could, anxiety rising. "His paternal grandfather had cancer. I get nauseous with anesthesia," I rattled off as best I remembered about our family.

Evan was listening and finally pushed himself off the gurney to say with exasperation, "Mom, I'm *adopted*!"

It was our one funny memory from that day. Honestly, in the crisis of the moment, I had forgotten. He is so firmly grafted into my tree that my history seems like his. I believe this is how God sees us, so firmly grafted into his tree that his history becomes ours. The stories of Abraham, Isaac, and Jacob are my stories. The tales of Daniel, David, Ruth, and Rahab are my family lore. Now that I am adopted into his family and considered a coheir with Christ, their faith is where I come from. "Look to the rock from which you were cut and to the quarry from which you were hewn" the prophet Isaiah challenged us (Isa. 51:1). I *am* in this community, and by design, the more I identify with it, the stronger I will be.

The Bible calls the community that goes before us the "great cloud of witnesses" (Heb. 12:1). They fought battles and stood firm. They trusted when it was hard and let go, surrendering to a plan written long ago. They embraced this live-amen theology in ways that leave me breathless, and we'll finish our time together honoring their example.

> Now faith is confidence in what we hope for and assurance about what we do not see. This is what the ancients were commended for. . . .
>
> By faith Abel brought God a better offering than Cain did. By faith he was commended as righteous, when God spoke well of his offerings. And by faith Abel still speaks, even though he is dead.
>
> By faith Enoch was taken from this life, so that he did not experience death: "He could not be found, because God had

taken him away." For before he was taken, he was commended as one who pleased God. And without faith it is impossible to please God, because anyone who comes to him must believe that he exists and that he rewards those who earnestly seek him.

By faith Noah, when warned about things not yet seen, in holy fear built an ark to save his family. By his faith he condemned the world and became heir of the righteousness that is in keeping with faith.

By faith Abraham, when called to go to a place he would later receive as his inheritance, obeyed and went, even though he did not know where he was going. By faith he made his home in the promised land like a stranger in a foreign country; he lived in tents, as did Isaac and Jacob, who were heirs with him of the same promise. For he was looking forward to the city with foundations, whose architect and builder is God. And by faith even Sarah, who was past childbearing age, was enabled to bear children because she considered him faithful who had made the promise. And so from this one man, and he as good as dead, came descendants as numerous as the stars in the sky and as countless as the sand on the seashore.

All these people were still living by faith when they died. They did not receive the things promised; they only saw them and welcomed them from a distance, admitting that they were foreigners and strangers on earth. People who say such things show that they are looking for a country of their own. If they had been thinking of the country they had left, they would have had opportunity to return. Instead, they were longing for a better country—a heavenly one. Therefore God is not ashamed to be called their God, for he has prepared a city for them.

By faith Abraham, when God tested him, offered Isaac as a sacrifice. He who had embraced the promises was about to sacrifice his one and only son, even though God had said to him, "It is through Isaac that your offspring will be reckoned." Abraham reasoned that God could even raise the dead, and so in a manner of speaking he did receive Isaac back from death.

By faith Isaac blessed Jacob and Esau in regard to their future. By faith Jacob, when he was dying, blessed each of Joseph's sons, and worshiped as he leaned on the top of his staff.

By faith Joseph, when his end was near, spoke about the exodus of the Israelites from Egypt and gave instructions concerning the burial of his bones.

By faith Moses' parents hid him for three months after he was born, because they saw he was no ordinary child, and they were not afraid of the king's edict.

By faith Moses, when he had grown up, refused to be known as the son of Pharaoh's daughter. He chose to be mistreated along with the people of God rather than to enjoy the fleeting pleasures of sin. He regarded disgrace for the sake of Christ as of greater value than the treasures of Egypt, because he was looking ahead to his reward. By faith he left Egypt, not fearing the king's anger; he persevered because he saw him who is invisible. By faith he kept the Passover and the application of blood, so that the destroyer of the firstborn would not touch the firstborn of Israel.

By faith the people passed through the Red Sea as on dry land; but when the Egyptians tried to do so, they were drowned.

By faith the walls of Jericho fell, after the army had marched around them for seven days.

By faith the prostitute Rahab, because she welcomed the spies, was not killed with those who were disobedient.

And what more shall I say? I do not have time to tell about Gideon, Barak, Samson and Jephthah, about David and Samuel and the prophets, who through faith conquered kingdoms, administered justice, and gained what was promised; who shut the mouths of lions, quenched the fury of the flames, and escaped the edge of the sword; whose weakness was turned to strength; and who became powerful in battle and routed foreign armies. Women received back their dead, raised to life again. There were others who were tortured, refusing to be released so that they might gain an even better resurrection. Some faced jeers and flogging, and even chains and imprisonment. They were put to death by stoning; they were sawed in two; they were killed by the sword. They went about in sheepskins and goatskins, destitute, persecuted and mistreated—the world was not worthy of them. They wandered in deserts and mountains, living in caves and in holes in the ground.

These were all commended for their faith, yet none of them received what had been promised, since God had planned something better for us so that only together with us would they be made perfect. (Heb. 11)

*And so amen. If you'll ask me to administer justice and conquer kingdoms, so be it. If you rescue me from flames and swords and enemies abound, I'll credit you. There is a better resurrection ahead. Amen. There is a communion with you I'll prefer to any other. I confess my sins. Forgive me, amen. I adore you, your ways, your plans, your nearness. Where you go, I'll go. I'll struggle along the way, but I trust you'll give me what I need. Oh, dear Jesus . . .*

He who testifies to these things says, "Yes, I am coming soon."

Amen. Come, Lord Jesus.

—REVELATION 22:20

# ACKNOWLEDGMENTS

This book was forming in my head during a trip I took to Turkey and Israel with Ray Vander Laan and That the World May Know Ministries. As anyone who knows me will attest, I am grateful beyond words for Ray's insights, which I hope I've honored here.

I am a spoke in a large wheel and am grateful for the ministry team I labor alongside. Whether you are in India, Nigeria, Haiti, Mexico, or Mason, Back2Back team, I appreciate how you offer your gifts and make sacrifices. These are lessons I've learned from you and alongside you. Jenna, our fruit hangs off the same tree. Thank you for how you model for me service. "I'm in if you're in." #iiiyi

I have dear friends who span over countries, decades, and age gaps. We've had experiences so rich that I feel ridiculously grateful to understand substance always counts over style. You have listened to me, come for me, and grown me up. Thank you for how you love well.

To Bryan Norman, thank you for the unwavering

commitment you've shown to me. I would've done this whole exercise just to now call you friend. To everyone at Alive and to Em for introducing me, I feel blessed to have been connected to you.

To Joel, Meaghan, and the W team, I appreciate your taking a chance on a girl with a journal full of stories and a heart to tell the truth about her spirituality. Happy to be in this family.

To my kids, I know there are costs and benefits to having a mom who tells stories. Thank you for counting the cost and sharing with me in the benefit. I am grateful we walk together in this journey of trusting God. You have taught me over and over again that love makes a family.

To Todd, like the lyric from your favorite song, it's always been you and I. Thank you for always working to really see me.

# NOTES

## Definition
1. *Oxford Dictionaries: English*, s.v. "amen," accessed September 22, 2016, http://www.oxforddictionaries.com/us/definition/american_english/amen.

## Prologue
1. Susan Hillis, James Mercy, Adaugo Amobi, Howard Kress, "Global Prevalence of Past-Year Violence Against Children: A Systematic Review and Minimum Estimates," *Pediatrics*, January 2016, http://pediatrics.aappublications.org/content/early/2016/01/25/peds.2015-4079.

## Chapter 1: So Be It
1. Flavius Josephus, *The Jewish War* 6.9.3.

## Chapter 4: The Barriers to Amen
1. "Turkey's Declining Christian Population," BBC, November 28, 2014, http://www.bbc.com/news/world-europe-30241181.

## Chapter 8: Mephibosheth and a Generous King

1. David Maxwell Braun, "Elephants Make the Earth Move with Seismic 'Love Calls,'" *National Geographic* (blog), February 14, 2009, http://voices.nationalgeographic.com/2009/02/14/elephants _make_the_earth_move/.

## Chapter 9: It's Better to Give Away a Life Than to Build One

1. *Oxford Pocket Dictionary of Current English*, s.v. "preemptive," Encyclopedia.com, accessed September 27, 2016, http://www .encyclopedia.com/humanities/dictionaries-thesauruses-pictures -and-press-releases/preemptive.

## Chapter 11: Rebuilding of Walls and Ruins

1. Amy Wilson-Carmichael, *Things as They Are: Mission Work in Southern India* (New York: Young People's Missionary Movement, 1906), 41–43.

# ABOUT THE AUTHOR

**B**eth Guckenberger and her husband, Todd, live with their family in Cincinnati, Ohio, where they serve as co-executive directors of Back2Back Ministries. After graduating from Indiana University, the Guckenbergers moved to Monterrey, Mexico, where they lived for fifteen years. Between biological, foster, and adopted children, they have raised ten children.

Beth is the author of seven books, including adult and children's titles. She travels and speaks regularly at conferences, youth gatherings, and church services. Her style is based in storytelling, and she draws from her vast field experience as a missionary, Bible teacher, and parent for illustrations of biblical concepts.